SUCCESS WITH
ORGANIC
VEGETABLES

SUCCESS WITH
ORGANIC VEGETABLES

Yvonne Cuthbertson

GUILD OF MASTER CRAFTSMAN
PUBLICATIONS LTD

For my good friend Sue Montague

First published 2006 by
Guild of Master Craftsman Publications Ltd
166 High Street, Lewes, East Sussex, BN7 1XU

Text © Yvonne Cuthbertson 2006
© in the Work GMC Publications Ltd

Illustrations by Penny Brown
Photographs © Yvonne Cuthbertson

ISBN -13 978-186108-478-1
ISBN -10 1-86108-478-1

British Cataloguing in Publication Data
A catalogue record of this book is available from the British Library

A catalogue record of this book is available from the British Library

Production Manager: Hilary MacCallum
Managing Editor: Gerrie Purcell
Editor: Alison Howard
Managing Art Editor: Gilda Pacitti
Designer: Jo Patterson

Set in Futura

Colour origination by Altaimage
Printed by and bound by Kyodo, Singapore

FOREWORD

Most amateur gardeners like the thought of being 'organic', and they usually start off in the right way. But as for anyone giving up a habit, giving up using chemicals in the garden requires a steely will. At the first sight of greenfly, the temptation to get the latest off-the-shelf convenient bug-blasting chemical can be all-consuming. But no! To be really organic you should pinch out the new growth harbouring the insects, or spray with a soap-based solution so staying there is unpleasant for them. If the infestation is severe, you may resort to an approved environmentally-friendly pesticide created from plant extract. Introducing some pests to predatory wasps, mites, nematodes and bacterium can also be an efficient and sensible control. Yes, there are always organic alternatives, and I implore every gardener to try them.

I reckon that gardeners who have an almost religious devotion to using chemicals should take time out. They should take a deep breath, and exist for just one year without using any form of conventional man-made chemical poison, and see what happens. Yes, there may be a few more insects around. Yes, the odd tomato or pepper may have to be discarded. But vigilance and a desire to protect the environment are strong weapons in the war against pests, and the satisfaction of knowing you've created something good, without leaving a dirty great footprint on the world in doing it, is extremely liberating.

I was delighted to read the manuscript, and applaud Yvonne Cuthbertson for writing this book. It should set any conventional vegetable gardener on the right course to becoming 'organic'. It will also serve as a great reminder to existing environmentalists that vegetables need quite specific attention if you are to get the best from them organically. I have been gardening organically myself for more than 10 years, but no-one ever knows it all, and some of Yvonne's tips have already found their way into my veg-growing regimes.

GRAHAM CLARKE MIHort, FLS
Consultant contributor to *Organic Life* magazine

Contents

LEFT **Flowers and vegetables growing together on a sunny terrace**

ABOVE A flower has developed on a courgette plant

Introduction

Organic gardening is not rocket science, it is simply a way of working with, rather than against, nature. It relies on natural methods of controlling pests and diseases, embraces the use of recycled materials to maintain soil fertility, and helps to provide an alternative habitat for wildlife. The basic principles of organic gardening follow those found in nature and are likely to increase both the yield and quality of your produce. Vegetables grown organically are full of flavour, safe and free from chemicals.

Interest in organic vegetable gardening has been rekindled by the desire to grow, eat and enjoy the freshest produce possible. Professional growers need to achieve high yields, often at the expense of flavour, and there is often concern over their practices. One of the greatest joys of home-grown organic vegetables is their taste; they have a sweetness, crispness and freshness that cannot be equalled. They are also better for you. Vegetables begin to lose their vitamins as soon as they are harvested, so they should be eaten as fresh as possible.

Vegetables can be incorporated in any garden. If yours is small, you may need to grow them in more imaginative ways. The idea that vegetables are ugly and should be hidden away no longer applies. With a little imagination and flair, they can be incorporated in any garden. Runner beans, for example, are extremely decorative and look marvellous in flower beds, containers, or as a focal point of a potager.

Growing good vegetables takes time and experience. Every gardener should be prepared to work hard and not be discouraged by the occasional failure. Fresh produce needs year-round attention and commitment. It is also better to start small and build on your success than to attempt self-sufficiency from the start and fail.

The vast choice of vegetables now on offer includes interesting crops such as okra, Chinese mustard and mizuna greens. It is best to grow vegetables your family really enjoys, especially those that are difficult to obtain or expensive. Home-grown vegetables follow a natural pattern and may be available only during certain periods. Many can be stored or frozen, but the seasons may begin to dictate what you eat – a concept that is both intriguing and challenging.

Vegetables can be cultivated with more certainty than ever. Research has improved understanding of what to grow and how to grow it, and new varieties have increased resistance to pests and diseases. Seeds, tools and garden aids are better, and correct soil preparation and organic cultivation will help. Gardening catalogues and magazines are a good source of information.

Nobody has the perfect site for all vegetables, and weather and soil conditions make it difficult to predict what a packet of seed or row of plants will yield. Tomatoes will crop heavily after a warm, sunny summer but not after a cool, wet one. Germination also depends to some extent on the climate, though cloches, polytunnels, cold frames and sheeting can offer some protection. Each vegetable has its own demands and idiosyncrasies. As you become more experienced, you will learn what you can and cannot grow in your garden. This is part of the challenge of successful vegetable growing. Meet that challenge with confidence and you will become even more motivated and enthusiastic. Successfully raising and eating vegetables that are all your own work is one of life's greatest pleasures, and will bring you an unparalleled sense of achievement.

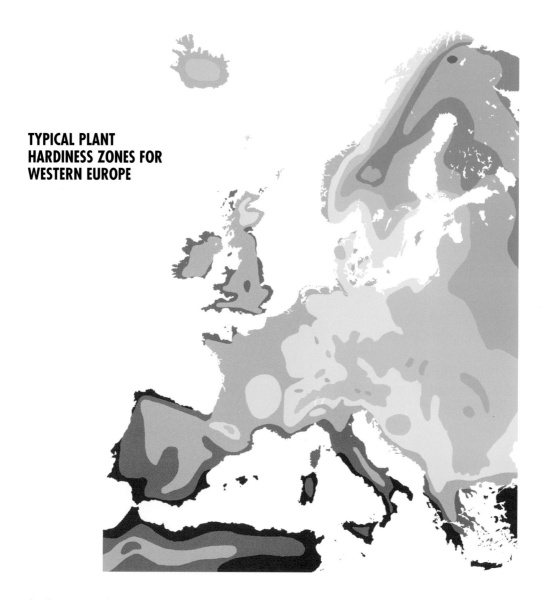

**TYPICAL PLANT
HARDINESS ZONES FOR
WESTERN EUROPE**

GROWING VEGETABLES ACROSS THE WORLD

Vegetables can be grown in many parts of the world. Conditions in some parts of Europe are similar to those found in Britain, so the same kinds of vegetables should grow happily. In other areas, including the Mediterranean, adjustments may be needed, including extra watering or planting in shade. Factors including extremes of cold and hours of sunlight must also be taken into account.

Across North America, there are more extreme variations of temperature than those found across Britain and Northern Europe. To grow vegetables successfully the factors that will need to be taken into consideration include the hours of cold weather in winter, how hot the summers are, and whether the climate is damp or dry. The charts on these pages should help you to determine your chances of success.

**TYPICAL PLANT
HARDINESS ZONES
FOR NORTH AMERICA**

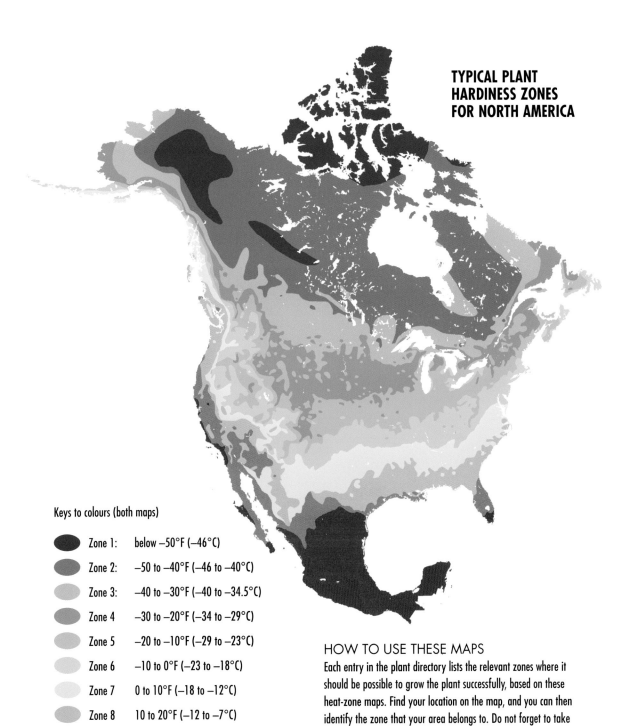

Keys to colours (both maps)

●	Zone 1:	below −50°F (−46°C)
●	Zone 2:	−50 to −40°F (−46 to −40°C)
●	Zone 3:	−40 to −30°F (−40 to −34.5°C)
●	Zone 4	−30 to −20°F (−34 to −29°C)
●	Zone 5	−20 to −10°F (−29 to −23°C)
●	Zone 6	−10 to 0°F (−23 to −18°C)
●	Zone 7	0 to 10°F (−18 to −12°C)
●	Zone 8	10 to 20°F (−12 to −7°C)
●	Zone 9	20 to 30°F (−7 to −1°C)
●	Zone 10	30 to 40°F (−1 to 4°C)
●	Zone 11	above 40°F (above 4°C)

HOW TO USE THESE MAPS

Each entry in the plant directory lists the relevant zones where it should be possible to grow the plant successfully, based on these heat-zone maps. Find your location on the map, and you can then identify the zone that your area belongs to. Do not forget to take into account that cities are warmer than rural locations. Planting shelter belts of trees, or planting against a sunny, south-facing wall and/or in raised, well-drained beds, can help to give plants better conditions in which to thrive.

11

LEFT A section of the vegetable garden
with forcing jars in the corner

13

CHAPTER 1

Where to grow vegetables outdoors

Vegetables can look as stunning as any of the decorative border plants, if the rigidity of the conventional kitchen garden is abandoned in favour of a more informal planting scheme. Delicious, fresh, home-grown vegetables are a vital part of the organic gardener's endeavours. Allow as much room as possible for growing them, and choose and cultivate them in a way that is aesthetically pleasing. In this way, the vegetable garden will be as one with the surrounding beds and borders.

ABOVE **A paved pathway through the vegetable garden**

CHOOSING YOUR SITE

Factors you must take into consideration include the area you are prepared to use and how best to fit it into the garden design. Take account of drainage, exposure to wind, and microclimate (diverse conditions that may be found in different areas of the garden). Decide whether you want your vegetables in full view of the house or patio, or would prefer them to be hidden away. Try to select a level piece of ground, or one that slopes toward the south to take full advantage of the sun. For vegetables to develop properly, it should provide at least six hours of full sun daily. Avoid low sites where frost strikes harder, try to avoid areas with poor drainage and make sure you are near a water source.

The ideal site should be open but not exposed or overshadowed by trees, hedges, walls or buildings. Soil should be fertile and well-drained with beds or rows running north-south, so taller plants do not shade crops below. Hedges and the roots of trees can deprive your crops of moisture and essential nutrients, and the soil beneath walls is prone to drying out. Sites that are too sheltered can promote the build-up of pests and diseases, but some low shelter is good as it increases air and soil temperatures. South-facing walls are a bonus as early crops can be raised at their foot in spring, and sun-loving plants like tomatoes and peppers grown against them in summer.

COPING WITH DIFFICULT SITES

A sloping site is more difficult to work than a flat one, although a gentle slope to the south is ideal. Very steep slopes are difficult to manage and can suffer from soil erosion: heavy rain washes the topsoil down to the bottom of the slope, leaving very little at the top. It also washes down nutrients so the upper soil becomes deficient in plant foods. Steep slopes can be very dry, as rain just runs straight down to the bottom. Digging is also a problem, as it

ABOVE A sunny corner of the vegetable garden

will be necessary to throw the soil uphill, a heavy and tiring process. Setting the vegetable beds across a slope may help, as may terracing the site to produce a series of flat surfaces. If you decide to do this, remove the topsoil and set aside before the work begins, then replace it when work is completed. The terraces can be retained using various materials including railway sleepers, bricks or logs. You might also consider building a brick retaining wall to either match or complement your house. If you cannot create terraces, mulching the plants with black polythene sheeting will help to check soil erosion, nutrient leaching and dry conditions.

WINDBREAKS

Vegetables grow best in a sunny, sheltered site, well-protected from winds – such protection can increase yields by up to one third. Gales can blow over tall crops like Brussels sprouts and rip the leaves of a lot of vegetables to pieces. Crops such as swedes, turnips, leeks, potatoes, kales and kohl rabi, however, do not particularly mind exposed areas. Hedges and fences will give protection from wind, provide a degree of privacy and establish boundaries, as will greenhouses, polytunnels, cold frames and cloches. But, if your site is exposed, you should think in terms of erecting windbreaks.

Vegetables grow better when they are protected from the drying and buffeting effect of wind. Windbreaks provide shelter at a distance equal to around five times their height, and full use should be made of natural windbreaks such as trees and hedges as well as fences and walls. Dripping and shading can create problems, as can competition for soil, water and plant nutrients. Tall plants like Jerusalem artichokes can make temporary windbreaks.

If there are no natural windbreaks in convenient places, erect artificial ones. Wind will be forced over solid structures, causing turbulence on the other side, so make sure wind can filter through. Netting battened to posts is ideal for the smaller garden. For the best effect windbreaks should be 39in (1m) high and 19ft 6in (6m) apart. As a short-term measure, low netting windbreaks about 18in (45cm) high can be constructed between rows of plants or beds. Attach ½in (12mm) netting to canes and place 9ft 9in–13ft (3–4m) apart. Hessian is even more effective.

DRAINAGE

In winter, badly-drained soil is likely to become waterlogged. One of the signs of poor drainage is when water lies on the surface of the soil for several days after a period of rain. The water forces air from the soil, so plant roots are drowned. Double-digging can help, as it breaks up the subsoil and lets water to pass through, but it will help only if there is somewhere for the water to flow. Raised beds can also help.

ABOVE **Screen netting can make a good temporary windbreak**

Indications of bad drainage include poor vegetation, a lack of earthworms, small shallow roots on plants, and greyish, bluish or mottled soil. The topsoil could be poor, for example, clay soil with little organic matter. Bulky organic material forked in will encourage worm activity and absorb a great deal of water, helping to solve the problem. If the problem persists, dig trench drains 12in (30cm) wide and 2–3ft (60–90cm) deep on either side of a level site or across the lower end of a slope. Fill the bottom end of the newly-dug trench with stones and clinkers before the soil is replaced. This should ease the problem, as the trench will usually absorb the water and allow the soil to become more workable. A soakaway (see right) dug at the lowest point may also help.

MICROCLIMATE

Altitude, latitude and degree of exposure will determine what can be grown outdoors in various localities. Most vegetables require an average daytime temperature between spring and autumn in excess of 43°F (6°C). Vegetable plants also vary in response to day length at various stages of growth. To decide which crops to plant and where to plant them, ask yourself these questions:

1 What is the position of my garden in relation to the sun?
2 How much sun does each area of my garden receive at various times of the day?
3 Which areas are in sun and shade at various times of the year?
4 Is any area particularly windy, and from which direction does the prevailing wind – if any – come?
5 Are any areas particularly exposed or sheltered?
6 Do any areas dry out completely in summer?

CONSTRUCTING A SOAKAWAY

1 Dig a hole at least 2ft (60cm) square and 3ft (90cm) deep at the lowest point in the garden.

2 Fill it to within 12in (30cm) of the top with rubble or large stones.

3 Cover with a 6in (15cm) layer of gravel or coarse sand.

4 Finish with a 6in (15cm) layer of topsoil to ground level.

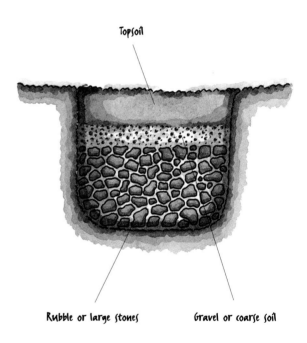

Topsoil

Rubble or large stones   Gravel or coarse soil

NEW GARDENS

If you have moved into a new house, you may find the builders have left rubble, bricks and debris behind, and that the soil is hard and compacted because heavy machinery, diggers and lorries have been driven over it. There may not be any topsoil in which to grow plants and you may have to buy some. But there is an advantage: with a new garden, you can select the best possible area in which to grow your crops and to screen it, if you so wish, from your ornamental garden.

It may be tempting to plant immediately, but you must resist until the ground has been adequately prepared. First, double-dig the area (see page 78) to break up the hard ground. Add plenty of organic matter to the trenches as you work. Remove perennial weeds like nettles, dandelions and docks, and any rubble and debris. Salvage bricks or slabs to use as foundations for paths and patios. Try to obtain a medium to light loam; you will need a depth of at least 30cm (12in) for vegetables.

PLOT SIZE

A plot about 95 x 32ft (30 x 10m), when it is systematically cropped, will provide vegetables for a family of four – apart from maincrop potatoes which take up a lot of space. You will need an even larger area to grow both early and maincrop potatoes. In the small gardens found today, a plot this size may not be possible. Maintaining a productive vegetable plot can also be time-consuming.

Make maximum use of limited facilities, and remember that crops can be grown cottage garden style in flower beds, in window boxes, on window sills and in containers. Deciding what you want to grow, and how much, will determine the size of your plot. It should also guarantee success, and provide the experience, confidence and incentive to progress to a bigger plot. If you are new to vegetable gardening, start with a small plot just 10 x 13ft (3 x 4m), and limit the number and variety of the vegetables you grow.

ABOVE **Cottage-style group of potted vegetables, herbs and flowers**

PLANNING YOUR PLOT

As for any other area of your garden it is necessary to draw up a plan. The size, shape and the nature of your garden and, of course, what you want to grow, will determine its layout. Your ideas must be practical or failure will follow. Consider how you will supply water. In a small garden, it is better to grow a few of many different types of vegetable. Avoid overplanting: one clump of rhubarb, for example, is enough for most families. Ask yourself these questions:

1 What produce do I want to grow?

2 What produce am I prepared to buy?

3 How much room is there in the freezer?

4 Which vegetables does the family like?

5 How much time am I willing to spend in the vegetable garden?

ABOVE **Crops planted in rows in the vegetable plot**

YOU WILL NEED
Plain paper
Graph paper
Pencil
Ruler

1 Decide what you want to grow by consulting seed catalogues and your family. List your choices in four groups: brassicas; root crops; legumes and other vegetables, plus a fourth group of any 'permanent' vegetables, such as asparagus and rhubarb, that you want to grow.

2 Draw your plot on graph paper, marking in static features such as the greenhouse, compost heap, or cold frame. Mark trees, walls, hedges and bonfire or incinerator site.

3 Divide the plot into four sections, using three sections for rotation crops, and the fourth for permanent crops. Mark in the paths.

4 Indicate rows or blocks of plants in each section, allowing space between them. On level ground, run rows north to south so the plants benefit from maximum sunlight. On a sloping site, plan rows to follow its contours. Place tall crops on the north side so they do not shade lower-growing plants as they mature.

VEGETABLE GARDEN DESIGNS

These plots are planned to look like letters of the alphabet or geometric shapes. Children love to see these fun designs in the garden, and with a little ingenuity, you can design your own. It helps if you draw out the shapes on graph paper first.

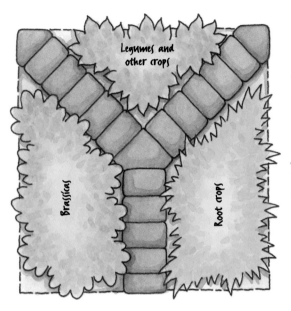

ABOVE **This vegetable garden design is in the shape of a letter Y, with paths made from paving slabs**

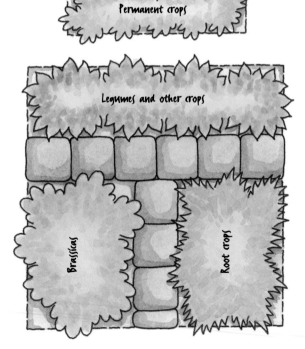

RIGHT **This vegetable garden design is in the shape of a letter T, with paths made of red brick**

GEOMETRIC SHAPES

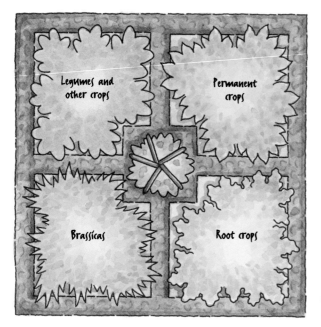

LEFT This design has paths of chipped bark and a runner bean wigwam as a focal point

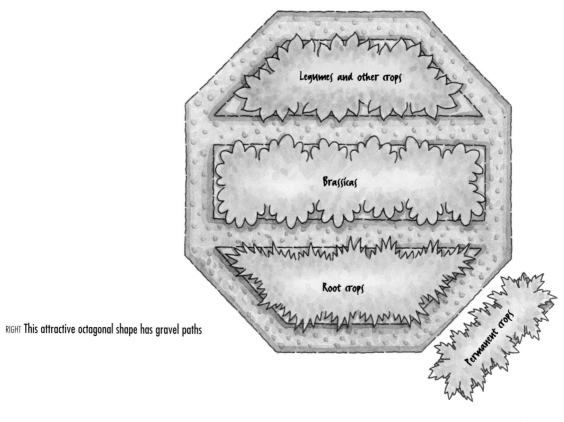

RIGHT This attractive octagonal shape has gravel paths

CIRCULAR DESIGN

A circular vegetable garden with paths of paving slabs and a focal point of herbs and flowers is an unusual way of growing vegetables that can provide a bold feature in your garden. It consists of circles linked by paving slabs, with the permanent crops accommodated in a smaller circle on one side of the outer path. It is easy to construct by tracing out two circles, one slightly smaller than the other. The circumferences will depend on how much ground is designated for the design. Use two short wooden stakes and string on a site that has been thoroughly prepared. Once they are laid, the paving stones will allow you to move around the area in all weathers, and the design is ideal for easy maintenance.

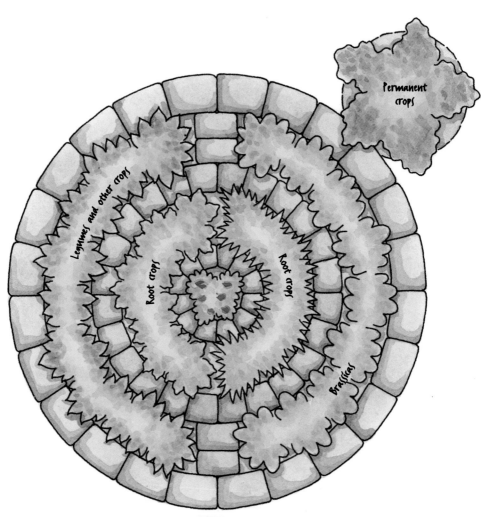

ABOVE An easily-maintained circular design with slab paths and a focal point of herbs and flowers

SALAD CROP CARTWHEEL

Use an old cartwheel to make an unusual small vegetable plot that will be a real talking point. If you do not have an old wheel, the instructions below will create a convincing replica.

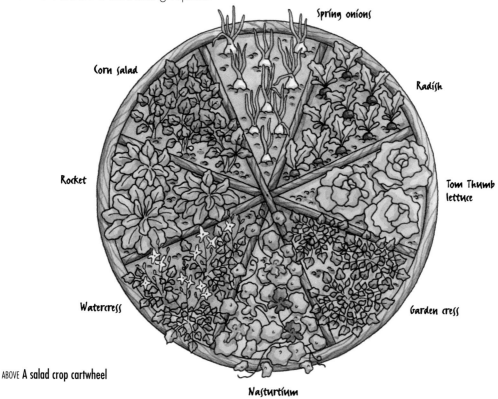

Spring onions

Corn salad

Radish

Rocket

Tom Thumb lettuce

Watercress

Garden cress

Nasturtium

ABOVE **A salad crop cartwheel**

MAKING A REPLICA CARTWHEEL

1 Separate the log rolls from the holding wires and paint with preservative and exterior varnish. Decorate the flower pot to match.
2 Mark out a circle on prepared ground using the stakes and string.
3 Remove some of the topsoil and place on a sheet of polythene. Loosen the subsoil.
4 Place the flower pot at the centre of the circle
5 Use the timber to divide the circle into eight segments. Tap in place using the mallet.
6 Position the edging logs and tap in firmly.
7 Replace some of the topsoil in each segment.
8 Plant each segment and water well.

YOU WILL NEED

Log rolls – number depends on wheel size
Flower pot for 'hub'
8 x lengths of 2 x 1in (5 x 2.5cm) timber for the wheel divisions
String and stakes
Wooden mallet
Selection of plants

RIGHT **The replica cartwheel**

MAKING A LETTUCE LADDER

1 Prepare an area of ground long and wide enough to accommodate the ladder.

2 Allow an extra 12–24in (30–60cm) at each side for companion plants.

3 Bed the ladder firmly into the ground.

4 Plant small varieties of lettuce (see list, right) in the spaces between the rungs.

5 Plant each side of the ladder with nasturtiums at intervals of 12in (30cm). Add some lobelia 'Crystal Palace' for an attractive contrast.

SUITABLE TYPES OF LETTUCE

'Little Gem' is a fast-maturing cos variety
'Mini Green' is a miniature crisphead
'Frisby' is a compact, loose-leaved lettuce
'Lollo Rosso' has attractive, frilly leaves
'Red Salad Bowl' is an endive-like variety
  with reddish-brown leaves
'Blush' is an attractive lettuce that has outer
  leaves flushed with pink
'Tom Thumb' has heads that are the size
  of tennis balls

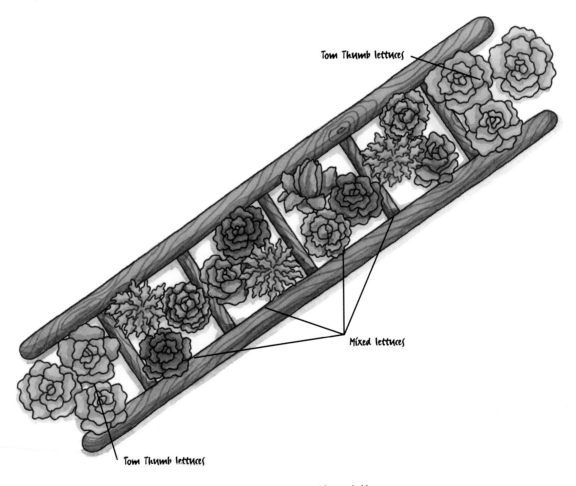

ABOVE **A lettuce ladder**

ABOVE **Positioning the ladder in the soil**

ABOVE **Planting 'Little Gem' lettuce in the ladder**

ABOVE **The lettuce ladder just after planting, with nasturtiums and obelia planted at the side**

ABOVE **Lettuce ladder with the plantings starting to mature**

LEFT **Lettuce ladder almost ready for harvesting**

25

ORIENTAL VEGETABLE PLOT

This is a novel and attractive way to grow a variety of interesting vegetables. A plot measuring 12 x 12ft (3.6 x 3.6m) is divided into nine sections using narrow paths made from recycled wood. These sections are surrounded by an 18in (45cm) wide border of chipped bark, and finished off with decorative log roll.

ABOVE **Oriental vegetable plot with paths of recycled wood and a Garland chrysanthemum as a focal point**

RAISED BEDS

These overcome the problem of heavy, infertile, badly drained soil, and are a good way to grow vegetables in a small garden. They can be free-standing, or built against a wall. Protect the wall with polythene sheeting to avoid damp.

Raised beds can be as little as 4in (10cm) above ground level. They can be used to divide the vegetable plot into compartments for easier crop rotation. Plants can be grown close together, reducing weeds and producing high yields of small vegetables. If organic matter is added, in time a deep layer of fertile soil develops. Crops can be forked, hoed, planted and harvested without treading on the soil and compacting it. Anchor fleece to the edges to protect early crops from frost, or netting to keep birds and butterflies away.

Make raised beds from recycled wood or rows of brick or stone set at an angle. They should be no more than 4ft (1.2m) wide, with narrow paths between them for easy access. Use chipped bark, gravel, or paving stones. Straw paths can be forked up and dug into beds at the end of the season, used as mulch in the second season, or added to the compost heap.

MAKING A RAISED BED

1 Level the site. Remove weeds. Mark out the shape of the beds using pegs and string. Check with a spirit level.

2 Hammer 15in (37.5cm) wooden posts into the corners, leaving about 4–5in (10–12.5cm) above ground level.

3 Cut lengths of board to fit between the posts. Nail in position and settle them into the soil. Check that the tops are even.

4 Lay straw down on the paths. Double-dig the bed, adding lots of well-rotted organic material.

ABOVE **An area cleared and ready for making a raised bed**

ABOVE **A raised bed ready for filling with compost**

ABOVE **A raised bed of mixed flowers and vegetables**

POTAGERS

Gardeners are becoming increasingly aware of how attractive their vegetable gardens can look, and a well-planted potager creates wonderful patterns of colour and foliage to stimulate the senses. A potager (which is French for kitchen garden) is an ornamental vegetable garden used to grow aesthetically-appealing crops like red lettuces and Swiss chard. The layout is similar to that of a parterre with formal beds and geometric patterns. If space is limited, a potager 10–13ft (3–4m) long will produce a reasonable range and quantity of produce.

Potagers are traditionally rectangular with beds planted with a mixture of vegetables, herbs, flowers and fruit. Paths run through and meet in the centre, which is the focal point of the design. A wigwam of runner beans (which have brilliant scarlet flowers), sweet peas and nasturtiums makes a stunning centrepiece. Globe artichokes surrounded by a circle of dwarf box can be very striking. Adding a few herbs such as golden marjoram, lemon balm and sage with its purple flowers adds impact to the design. Diagonal planting enhances the aesthetic appeal, and a companion-planted flower border of marigolds and nasturtiums will deter pests. A potager will also benefit from a surrounding low, box hedge, though a certain amount of patience will be necessary as box is notoriously slow growing.

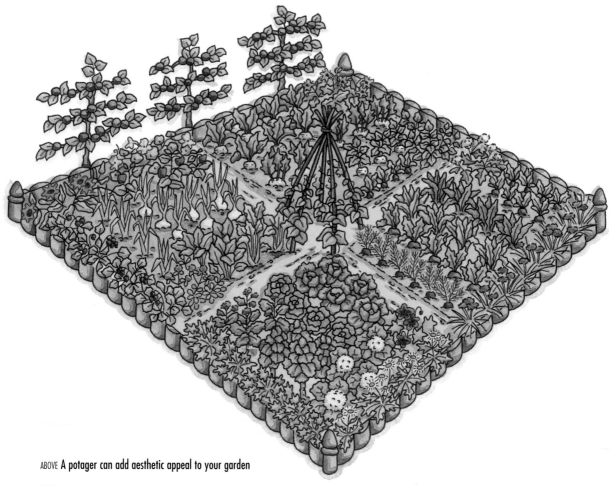

ABOVE **A potager can add aesthetic appeal to your garden**

ABOVE **Aubergines 'Long Tom' growing in the flower border**

Start planning your potager by choosing your site and deciding on your design and which plants and crops you intend to use. Draw a scaled plan that includes your design and plant placements, windbreaks, ornamental features and pathways. Mark it out using pegs and string, allowing paths about 2ft (60cm) wide for easy access.

To produce succulent crops, your potager will need fertile soil (pH5.5–6.5). Double-dig each bed, adding lots of organic material. Maximise crop production by spacing plants densely, intercropping with fast-growing plants. Planting in succession will prolong availability and avoid gluts. Remember that when produce is harvested, there will be gaps left. It is bad gardening practice to grow the same crops in an area of ground each year; the crops will be rotated, so it will not be possible to use exactly the same pattern every year.

THE FLOWER BORDER

Growing vegetables in the flower border is both attractive and productive. It will attract lots of beneficial insects, such as ladybirds and hoverflies – which will eat large numbers of aphids and prevent them from attacking your crops – into your garden. Border-planted vegetables must be grown and cared for in the same way as those in the vegetable plot. Plant spreading vegetables, such as pumpkins and courgettes, singly. Grow other vegetables in irregular-shaped drifts.

Vegetables can complement flowers, so choose plants with interesting or colourful foliage: red lettuce, Swiss chard or purple cabbage, for example. The feathery foliage of asparagus makes an excellent foil for border flowers, and a mix of nasturtiums and edible cabbages is attractive. Pumpkins 'Baby Bear' can be trailed along a fence, and cordon

ABOVE **A wigwam of organic runner beans**

CONTAINERS

If you do not have enough ground to grow the vegetables you need, most crops will succeed in containers, fed and watered regularly to maximise yields. There are positive benefits from growing produce in containers: they can be moved to a sunny position to protect them from the cold, and they attract fewer soil pests. Compost and drainage can be adjusted to suit different plants. For the best results, use as large a container as possible. A single small vegetable such as a lettuce will need a pot at least 6in (15cm) wide in order to thrive. An 11in (28cm) container is ideal for one larger vegetable or four lettuces. Beans, cucumbers and tomatoes need a 13in (33cm) pot. Avoid shallow containers as the roots will not have enough depth, and the compost will dry out very fast, or become waterlogged.

All vegetables crop well in a multipurpose compost, but this can prove expensive in large quantities. It is cheaper to buy growing bags and tip out the contents, or add up to half the volume of garden topsoil to the compost. For an organic gardener, home-made compost from the compost heap is both ideal and free.

tomatoes can be trained up canes and placed at the back of the border, to one side for easy access. A wigwam of runner beans can look stunning, as can a selection of courgettes.

Try planting broad beans in the spring border, and use coloured lettuce as early border fillers. Winter vegetables, such as leeks, crinkly leaved Savoy cabbages, variegated chicory or some of the red or blue-grey leaved kales will brighten up a dull border when summer flowers have faded. Try planting rhubarb in the middle of your border and cardoons at the back. A striking edging can be achieved by planting chives, bright red beetroot or frilly lettuces.

ABOVE **A pair of old boots makes an unusual and attractive container**

ABOVE **An extensive range of pots**

CHOOSING POTS AND TUBS

The pots you choose will depend largely on your budget. Plastic pots are light in weight, relatively inexpensive, easy to store and clean, and will not crack when it is frosty. Water content can be judged simply by lifting them. Remember to make drainage holes before planting. Moulded polypropylene, mock terracotta pots look attractive and provide insulation for the compost.

Clay and terracotta pots are more expensive. They dry out more quickly than plastic pots, so will need to be watered more frequently or lined with polythene. They are also heavy. Soak new pots in water for twenty-four hours before using.

Glazed earthenware pots offer a great choice of colour and design, and the glazing prevents water loss. Not all glazed pots have drainage holes, so check before buying.

Concrete pots can be bought in a variety of designs and mouldings. They are extremely stable and frost-resistant, but are heavy to move around. They can take a long time to weather, making them rather bleak in appearance.

Reconstituted stone pots are made from stone that is ground up and then moulded into shape. They take a while to weather, and are heavy to move around, but are stable and frost-resistant.

Wooden half-barrels are stable, frost-resistant, and make stunning containers for mixed displays. They may fall apart if allowed to dry out, and you will probably need to drill drainage holes before planting. Replicas are available, but some have plywood bases and inferior metal bands so their lifespan is short.

Glass fibre containers are expensive, but modern and stylish. They have a high gloss finish, and come in a variety of colours, but may crack or shatter if knocked. They are more stable than plastic pots, frost-resistant, and relatively easy to move around.

PLANTING POTS AND TUBS

Use two parts of multipurpose compost to one part grit. Place a deep layer of hardcore at the bottom to ensure good drainage, weight and stability. Place large pieces over the drainage holes, then a layer of smaller pieces to a depth of at least 1in (2.5cm). Add a layer of peat or pulverized bark to prevent the compost washing away. Line containers with plastic sheeting to conserve water, or sink a bottomless upturned plastic bottle into the compost to allow water to penetrate the root. Place a layer of compost about 3in (7.5cm) deep over the peat or bark.

Always set tubs or troughs in their final positions before filling and planting. Informal planting is better than a regimented look. Walk round the container and view it from all angles. Use a trowel to fill the container to within 1in (2.5cm) of the top and dig planting holes for your crops. After planting, water well to help settle the compost. Use a fine rose and water the foliage to remove any soil particles. Water in the shade as the rays of the sun on wet leaves could damage them.

HANGING BASKETS

These provide immediate impact and add height to a planting scheme. Many types are available, but a popular choice is a round-bottomed, wire basket. It can be lined with various materials from sphagnum moss to preformed wood fibre liners. Wool 'moss' has excellent water-retaining properties, and makes a good substitute for natural moss.

METHOD

1 Stand the basket in a bucket or large pot to stop it moving. Line with moss or a liner and place a polythene disc in the bottom to help retain moisture.

2 Add a little multi-purpose compost and mix in some water-retaining granules.

3 Gently open any slits in the outside of the liner or make your own planting holes.

4 Insert one plant in each slit/hole. Fill with compost as you go, firming around each plant. Work from the inside if possible, and take care not to damage the root ball.

5 Build up in layers, working from the bottom up. Plant the outside of the basket first, then the top of the basket.

6 Water well and stand in a frost-free place to settle.

ABOVE **Peppers 'Hungarian Wax' grow well in a large pot**

AFTERCARE
Water daily and feed regularly. Trim any straggly growth and remove any dead leaves and debris.

SUGGESTED PLANTINGS

Tomatoes 'Tiny Tim'
Dwarf beans 'Firetongue' and French marigolds
French beans 'Purple Queen'

VEGETABLES FOR CONTAINER PLANTING

Compact, fast maturing plants like radishes, lettuces and beetroot or leafy vegetables such as spinach beet are best. Potatoes also grow well in containers. Many members of the Solanaceae family – aubergine, cape gooseberry, peppers, tomatillo and tomatoes flourish in containers and also look good. Dwarf cultivars are ideal as they need no support. Never use deep-rooted, slow-maturing vegetables or very tall or large varieties. Avoid gross feeders such as brassicas, parsnips and celery. Raise plants for containers in modules, but sow cut-and-come-again seedling crops directly into the containers.

SUGGESTIONS FOR CONTAINERS

- ◆ Mix vegetables and edible flowers like pot marigold and violas
- ◆ Grow Lollo Rosso lettuce with parsley, chives and coriander
- ◆ Plant lettuce, onions, beetroot, garlic and broad beans in a wooden half-barrel
- ◆ Fill a pot with small-fruiting peppers such as 'Tabasco' and 'Serrano'
- ◆ Mix watercress, garden cress and borage
- ◆ Grow tomatoes and basil together
- ◆ Plant parsley in the sides of a strawberry pot and aubergines in the crown
- ◆ Use thyme in the sides of a strawberry pot and 'Tumbling Tom' tomatoes in the crown
- ◆ Plant ruby chard in a large pot for a stunning effect
- ◆ Use chive flowers to add colour

ABOVE **Tomatoes can look stunning in a hanging basket**

WINDOW BOXES

These are available in various materials, including wood, terracotta and plastic. Wood can be painted or stained to complement the style of your house. Make sure the fixing used will take the weight of the box when full.

If you prefer to make your own window box to fit your sill exactly, choose treated hardwood such as elm, western red cedar, or oak, which is the most durable. It should have drainage holes. Line it with polythene sheeting and place a layer of crocks over the drainage holes. Use a multipurpose compost mixed with a little sharp sand and add water-retaining polymer granules. These absorb large amounts of moisture, which is released over a long time. Water regularly, and remove any dead leaves and debris. Feed at regular intervals throughout the summer. Treat the finished box with preservative.

STRAWBERRY POT

This is an attractive feature when planted with vegetables like tomatoes. Use a frost-resistant planter with good drainage and good-sized planting holes. Keep the compost moist and feed once a week from spring to late summer.

YOU WILL NEED
Terracotta strawberry pot
Compost
Strawberry plants
Thyme plants

1 Place hardcore in the bottom and add a layer of compost up to the bottom of the lowest hole.

2 Starting from the bottom, insert the plants in the side pockets. Fill with compost as you go, making sure there is room only for the rootball, with no empty spaces.

3 Continue to the top. Complete the pot with the crown planting.

4 Water the pot well to settle in the plants.

ABOVE **Tomato and thyme planted in a strawberry pot**

POTATOES IN A POT

Just-dug potatoes taste fantastic. If your garden is small, plant seed potatoes in a pot in spring. You will be amazed by the results. Use a strong, stable container at least 10in (25cm) wide and deep, to hold at least 9 pints (10 litres) of light soil/compost. Plastic containers conserve moisture better. Fill the bottom with about 6in (15cm) of compost or soil. Place 3–4 chitted seed potatoes (Pentland Javelin are ideal), buds uppermost, in the bottom of the pot and cover with 4–5in (10–12cm) more compost. Cover with more soil or compost as they sprout, just like earthing up potatoes in your garden. It will encourage the stems to produce a bigger crop.

Place the container in a sunny, sheltered spot and keep it well-watered; potatoes need lots of water. Fertilize the plants every two weeks with tomato feed. During hot weather, the crop may need watering twice a day. Move the container into the shade to prevent the compost drying out too quickly. By the end of summer the top growth will begin to die down, and the potatoes will be ready to harvest. Tip them out, clean away the compost and you will have a wonderful harvest of perfect, ready-to-eat potatoes.

ABOVE **Chit the seed potatoes by placing in an egg box or seed tray with the 'eyes' (dormant buds from where the shoots emerge) upwards. Keep in a cool, light place.**

YOU WILL NEED
Large container
3–4 chitted seed potatoes
Compost

1 Prepare the pot and soil ready to plant the potatoes

2 Add chitted seed potatoes and cover with compost. As the shoots emerge, add more compost until only the tips can be seen.

3 Repeat the process until the container is full to within 1–2in (2.5–5cm) of the rim.

4 Keep the potato plants watered as they grow.

5 Wait until the plants die off to harvest them.

6 Harvest the potatoes by tipping the container.

MAINTENANCE

Never let your pots and tubs dry out or become waterlogged, and keep your watering can filled so the water is at the same temperature as the atmosphere. Water containers even after rain, because the 'umbrella' of leaves may prevent water from reaching the compost, and the plants can wilt quite quickly. Apply an organic liquid feed once a fortnight during summer.

CHAPTER 2

Cultivating vegetables under cover

In cooler climates, productivity can be increased dramatically if crops are raised under cover. Cooler climates mean shorter growing seasons, and the shorter the growing season, the more effective a protected environment is likely to be. Air and soil temperatures are increased and crops are sheltered from the wind, which can prolong the growing season by up to eight weeks.

Crops can be started in early spring, then hardened off and planted outside when the temperatures rise. The winter cropping period may be lengthened, and higher temperatures and shelter will improve the quality and yield of many plants. Some half-hardy varieties of summer vegetable that will not mature outside during the growing season may do so if they are grown under cover.

ABOVE **A small greenhouse in a corner of the garden**

GREENHOUSES

These expand the growing season, so you can grow and harvest a variety of vegetables and salad crops much earlier than if they were in open ground. Plants can be kept in them permanently, or for just a short time before being moved to the vegetable plot. This flexibility will allow you to have an almost continual supply of vegetables, including carrots, lettuce, sweet peppers, beetroot and aubergines.

Organic principles lend themselves well to greenhouse culture. If you are going organic for the first time, dig out the soil from the beds in autumn to a depth of around 12in (30cm), break up the bottom using a fork, and replace with well-rotted, friable, organic compost. Dress the bed with blood, fish and bonemeal (about 5oz per sq yd /150g per sq m). Plant winter lettuces, carrots, radish and spring cabbage directly into the bed. In spring, add a top dressing of compost and more blood, fish and bonemeal. An application of seaweed will guard against potash shortage.

The soil in an organic greenhouse does not need to be replaced every year. When the crops have been harvested, remove the remains with plenty of compost attached, then fill the planting holes with fresh compost. In this way, the growing compost is continuously renewed without increasing the level of the bed. In the unlikely event of soil-borne pests or diseases, dig the compost out and replace with a fresh batch.

BUYING AND SITING A GREENHOUSE

Greenhouses come in a range of shapes and sizes to suit any garden, from the most common free-standing design to a lean-to placed against an existing wall. Choose the largest you can afford and have space for; the initial cost will soon be repaid. Aluminium is inexpensive, virtually maintenance free and easy to construct. Wood looks natural and retains more heat, but costs more and is high on maintenance.

ABOVE **A cucumber plant growing in the greenhouse**

Polycarbonate glazing is lighter and a better heat insulator than the traditional glass. Choose an open, sunny position and try to make the most of the sun by ensuring that the roof ridge runs from east to west, with the longest side to the south. There should be some shelter from wind, but make sure fences, walls, hedges or trees are not too near or they will cast shade. Trees will also drop leaves, which may exude gums that make the glazing dirty and are difficult to remove. Lean-to greenhouses should face as nearly south as possible to receive maximum light. The rear wall will store warmth during the day and release it at night.

You can use a greenhouse to raise early crops of many types of vegetable, including aubergine (eggplant), potatoes, cucumbers, early carrots, lettuce, radish, spinach, spring onions, tomatoes and turnips. The degree to

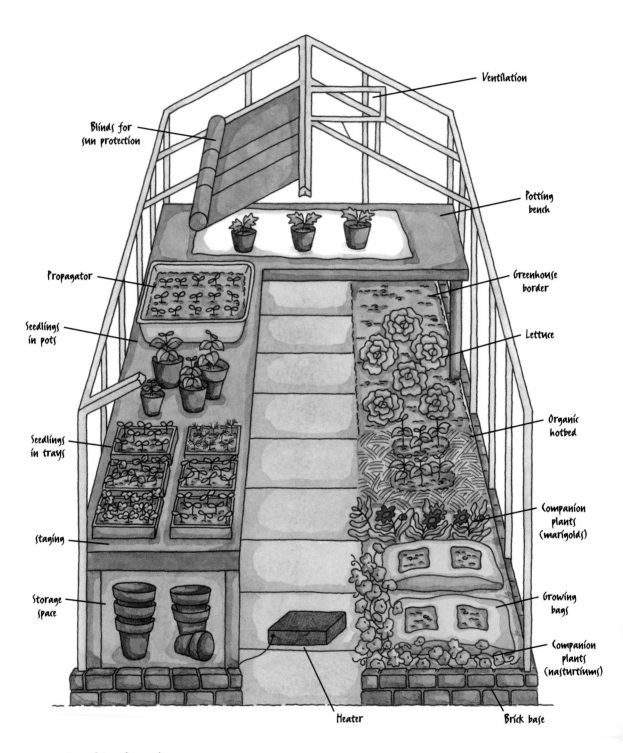

ABOVE Internal view of a greenhouse

40

which you heat your greenhouse will depend on what you want to grow. Most vegetables are grown in unheated or slightly heated greenhouses, so early yields can be produced economically. Attach sheets of bubble polythene to your glazing to reduce heat loss and complement your heating system.

If you want to over-winter tender plants heating is essential. Thermostatically-controlled electric heaters are reliable and clean, but remember to use a qualified electrician. Gas heaters can also work on a thermostat, but are more expensive to run. Paraffin heaters are ideal for keeping out frost, but not for constant use. Both gas and paraffin heaters give off water vapour, which can cause condensation.

GREENHOUSE PROPAGATORS

These are enclosed cases that have a built-in heating element, and are ideal if you want to sow tender crops, like tomatoes and peppers, early in the season. They help to reduce heating costs by restricting the area that has to be heated. Delicate crops can be overwintered and faster germination achieved when starting off vegetables. Keep your propagator moisture-free and wipe off condensation that has formed overnight so drips do not make the seedlings too wet or cause them to damp off.

GREENHOUSE TEMPERATURES

COLD GREENHOUSE
Minimum temperature: a few degrees warmer than outside

COOL GREENHOUSE
Minimum temperature: 40–45°F (5–7°C)

WARM GREENHOUSE
Minimum temperature: 55°F (13°C)

ABOVE **An unheated propagator**

WATERING

Too much moisture encourages botrytis and moulds; too little can encourage spider mite and mildew. During the growing season, err on the side of caution and spray the plants, floor and glass sides of your greenhouse with a fine jet of water. Spray in the morning so it will be dry before evening. Keep a tank of water under the staging and refill after watering so it is always at the same temperature as the greenhouse.

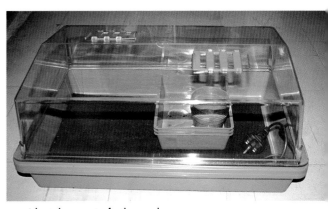

ABOVE **A heated propagator for the greenhouse**

41

SOIL-WARMING BENCH

This is a useful greenhouse extra, as heat at the roots is more important for newly-rooted plants than warm air around the tops. A suitable weather-proof electrical socket, installed by a qualified electrician, is essential.

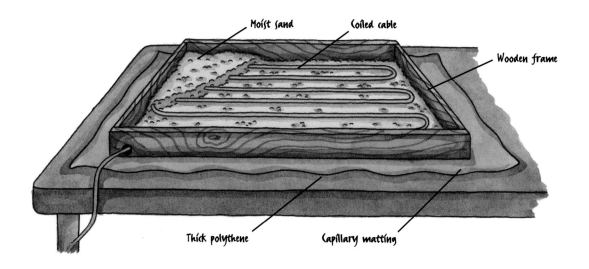

Moist sand   Coiled cable   Wooden frame

Thick polythene   Capillary matting

ABOVE **A soil-warming bench**

METHOD

1 Build a wooden frame to the size required, using 1 x 6in (2.5 x 15cm) timber treated with a plant-friendly preservative.

2 Drill a hole for the cable (for type and amount required, consult an electrician).

3 Cover a level bench with a layer of thick polythene and top with capillary matting.

4 Place the frame on top and fill with a 1in (2.5cm) layer of moist sand.

5 Coil the cable along the length of the bench so that all areas receive some heat. Leave 3–4in (7.5–10cm) between each run of cable to prevent overheating.

6 Cover the cable with a further 2–3in (5–7.5cm) of soft sand.

Note The sand must be kept moist at all times to prevent the cable from overheating, and to ensure that heat is transferred to the compost in the pots and trays placed on it.

LIGHT AND VENTILATION

Light is one of the most important factors of plant growth, and as much as possible should be let in. Good ventilation is vital for plant health and to control the inside temperature of your greenhouse. In sun, temperatures will soar unless air can circulate. In cold, dull weather, poor ventilation can cause humid, stale air that will give rise to plant diseases such as moulds and rots. Vents should be easy to open. Automatic vents that open when the temperature rises are inexpensive and simple to install. Removable side panels are a must. Keep the door open in summer as temperatures rise fast.

SHADING

The sun can scorch plants, so some sort of shading is wise. Special shading paint, available from DIY centres, can be applied in spring and wiped off in autumn. Shading panels that clip in place are available for some aluminium greenhouses. Other options are shading fabrics such as plastic netting or adjustable roller blinds.

STAGING, SHELVING AND BENCHING

Staging is often included in the price. It raises plants nearer to the light, ensuring healthy growth, and maximises space. It may be made from wood or aluminium, and can be slatted, solid, or mesh. Choose staging that has a second level just above the ground, which is ideal for over-wintering plants. Shelving can be fitted anywhere inside or round the outside of your greenhouse. Make sure it is deep enough and that there is enough space for a seed tray to sit on it. Benching is removable staging that can be folded away to increase floor space for growing bags or pots. Replace it at the end of the season to support over-wintering crops.

ABOVE **A greenhouse vent for allowing the air to circulate**

BELOW **The inside of a greenhouse showing aluminium slatted staging**

PESTS IN THE ORGANIC GREENHOUSE

Good husbandry is 90 per cent of successful organic gardening. Choosing plants that are generally problem-free and growing them well helps, but when the greenhouse ventilators or door are open, pests will find their way in.

Insects can be controlled organically by encouraging natural predators like ladybirds, lacewings, hoverflies, centipedes and black beetles. Plant a good selection of brightly-coloured, nectar- and pollen-rich flowers such as French marigolds to encourage beneficial insects. Tobacco plants are useful for controlling small insects such as thrips, which they trap on their sticky stems. Useful insects bought by mail order, can be introduced early in the season. Mealy bugs can be controlled using the larvae of the ladybird (ladybug) *Cryptolaemus montrouzieri*, aphids by the parasitic midge *Aphididoletes aphidmyza*, and whitefly by the parasitic wasp *Encarsia Formosa*. The naturally-occurring *Bacillus thuriengiensis* can be sprayed on crops to rid your greenhouse of caterpillars. See also Companion Planting, page 144.

COMMON GREENHOUSE PESTS
Ants
Birds
Caterpillars
Mice
Greenfly
Red spider mite
Scale insect
Slugs and snails
Vine weevil
Whitefly
Woodlice

DISEASES

Plant diseases are at their worst in early spring, autumn and winter when light levels are low and the air is cold and damp. Prevention is better than cure, so keep your greenhouse clean, tidy and ventilated. Remove dead or damaged material from the floor and dispose of it. Water plants in winter only when absolutely necessary. Avoid damping off in seedlings by sowing seed later in the spring.

COMMON GREENHOUSE DISEASES
Grey mould
Neck rot
Powdery mildew
Root rot
Damping off

LEFT **The inside of a greenhouse**

THE GREENHOUSE YEAR

SPRING
Ventilate the greenhouse during sunny days throughout spring, but keep it closed at night. Keep the atmosphere fairly dry.

Early spring
Continue to ventilate. Sow peppers, aubergines and cucumbers for cultivating in a cold greenhouse, and tomatoes for cloches.

Mid-spring
Increase ventilation and shade as necessary. Plant aubergine and pepper seedlings, and tomatoes in growing bags. Sow cucumbers to grow under cloches and leeks, okra, runner beans, celeriac and squashes to plant outside.

Late spring
Increase ventilation. Shade on very sunny days. Feed tomatoes and remove side-shoots.

SUMMER
Feed all fruiting vegetables weekly throughout summer. Damp down the greenhouse regularly.

Early summer
Paint on shading or let down the blinds. Increase ventilation. Remove tomato side-shoots. Start pinching out and training fruiting vegetables.

Mid summer
Repair and paint the greenhouse if necessary. Continue feeding and removing side-shoots from tomatoes and cucumbers. Begin harvesting.

Late summer
Continue with day and night ventilation. Start sowing winter lettuce in seed trays.

AUTUMN
Throughout the autumn, reduce ventilation and damping down.

Early autumn
Make sure greenhouse heaters are working. Continue sowing winter lettuce.

Mid-autumn
Start to close the greenhouse at night. Sow short-day lettuce in a cold greenhouse.

Late autumn
Begin to heat the greenhouse. Transplant short-day lettuce.

WINTER
Ventilate the greenhouse on sunny days. Adjust heating as necessary. Keep the atmosphere dry.

Early winter
Clean out and wash down the greenhouse.

Mid-winter
Begin heating the greenhouse for early sowing. Start sowing globe artichokes, turnips, onions, cucumbers, peppers, carrots, radishes, spinach and summer brassicas.

Late winter
Regulate heating as necessary. Start sowing tomatoes, celery, peas, aubergines, early spinach and sweet corn.

CLEANING THE GREENHOUSE

The closed atmosphere can encourage pests and diseases, so empty and clean your greenhouse thoroughly once a year. Scrub down the inside of the glass, the frame, staging, shelves and floor using warm water, detergent and a soft brush. Scrape off any moss or algae. Scrub the outside glass using clean water and a garden disinfectant, and rinse well with a strong jet of water. Leave the door and the ventilators open and let them dry before returning the plants. Scrub pots using hot water and detergent, and let them dry before stacking. Sterilize pots once a year using hot water and garden disinfectant.

ABOVE **Tomatoes growing in the greenhouse**

COLD FRAMES

Cold frames are low, semi-permanent structures with a sloping glazed top and glazed sides. They help to protect plants in winter and prevent them from becoming waterlogged. Choose a frame deep enough to accommodate the range of vegetables you wish to grow, that lets in plenty of light. Various designs are available, but modern cold frames usually have metal frames and glass all round. They also have a glass roof or 'light' that is either hinged or designed to slide back. Solid-sided frames retain the most heat, but not as much light. If more light is a priority, choose a glass-to-ground frame.

Most hardy vegetables will germinate without extra heat, but enjoy the protection of a cold frame. In winter, use them to protect crops such as lettuce, and in summer, tender crops like cucumber. They can be used to sow early vegetables such as carrots, lettuce and spring onions several weeks ahead. They are also useful for hardening off vegetables, ready to plant outside in early summer when all danger of frost has passed.

Do not put too many plants in a cold frame: they will shade each other as they grow, and the resulting weak, leggy plants will not withstand growing conditions in the open ground. Water well so humidity is maintained in the frame during the night.

Cold frames are almost airtight, so always ventilate them a little, both day and night. In mild, sunny weather, prop the glass roof, or 'light' open every morning to prevent heat build-up. Too much heat will stress plants, discolour their foliage and leave them vulnerable to pests. In closed frames, condensation and damp will build up and create conditions in which fungal diseases will thrive.

If you heat your cold frame, it can be used just like a tiny greenhouse to produce seedlings and grow vegetables over an extended season.

ABOVE **A paraffin heater for a cold frame**

FORCING CROPS IN A COLD FRAME

Cold frames can also be blacked out for forcing crops such as chicory and endive. In spring and summer, many seeds can be germinated and grown on in modules, trays or pots. For extra insulation, cover the cold frame with a blanket or piece of carpet at night and insulate the sides with polystyrene sheets cut to size with a knife.

HARDENING OFF IN A COLD FRAME

Plants must be kept growing smoothly to ensure success. Acclimatize greenhouse-raised plants gradually before you transfer them to the open ground. Put them into a closed cold frame a week or so before you intend to plant them out. Leave the frame closed for 24 hours. On the second day, open the top slightly, but close it at night. Gradually increase the size of the opening during the day until the top is removed completely, but keep it almost closed at night. Then begin to open the frame more at night until the top is off completely. The plants will now be ready to grow in open ground.

ABOVE **A cold frame**

POLYTUNNELS

Walk-in polytunnels provide warmth and humidity and are an excellent aid for growing vegetables. Less-hardy crops can be grown and two crops can be raised each year instead of one. Early potatoes, cabbages, cauliflowers, carrots, lettuce and spinach can be followed by peppers, cucumbers, aubergine (eggplant), sweetcorn (maize) and tomatoes. Polytunnels are also excellent for growing winter and early spring vegetables, propagating crops and housing them until they are ready to plant outside. However, the conditions inside can encourage fungus diseases such as moulds and rots, which particularly affect peppers, as well as pests like red spider mite, white fly and slugs.

Polytunnels are more airtight than greenhouses and retain heat accordingly. Provide extra ventilation in hot weather by cutting out small, low level vents along the sides, which can be taped back in winter. It is not feasible to heat a polytunnel, and the plastic film will need to be replaced after about three years.

Polytunnels are cheaper and easier to erect than a greenhouse. They are also relatively easy to move around to avoid pest and disease build-up in the soil. Buy the biggest you can afford and for which you have space. A wide tunnel will give more working space from the sides, and ventilation is better. The ridge should run from west to east so that the longest side gets the sun all day. Do not site it in heavy shade.

CHOOSING VEGETABLES TO GROW IN A POLYTUNNEL

Raise broad beans, Brussels sprouts, cabbage, sprouting broccoli, onions, celeriac, celery, kale, leeks and runner beans in a polytunnel, then transplant to open ground. Avoid artichokes, asparagus, maincrop potatoes, salsify, parsnips, shallots and swedes as these do not thrive in polytunnels.

ABOVE **A large commercial polytunnel**

CLOCHES

These are low, transparent portable covers that can be used to warm up and dry out ground before sowing or planting. Place cloches over a seedbed a couple of weeks before sowing and it will help to speed up germination.

Cloches also help transplanted crops to become established and extend the season into late autumn for vegetables such as lettuce. They protect crops from bad weather so it is possible to grow a wider range of vegetables and sometimes to harvest them earlier. They can be used to harden off greenhouse crops and protect crops from rabbits, birds and some insects.

Glass cloches are expensive, but plastic cloches will need replacing every few years. Small 'tent' cloches 12–18in (30–45cm) wide are for starting off seedlings or young plants, but plants will soon outgrow them. Tunnel or barn cloches are a better shape for more mature plants, or to cover a large area of crops.

Cloches can be placed end-to-end to cover a whole row of vegetables. Ventilate them on warm, sunny days, either by removing the whole cover, taking off the sides, or adjusting the flaps.

POLYTHENE FILM TUNNEL

This is the cheapest form of crop protection and a good alternative to a cloche. It is made from polythene sheeting that is stretched over wire hoops and secured with string or wires. It is easy to erect and move, and is ventilated by leaving the ends open or rolling up the sides. The polythene retains heat and transmits light well, but must be replaced whenever it becomes yellow or torn.

HORTICULTURAL FLEECE

This lightweight polypropylene fleece can be used to protect tender crops from the winter cold. It can lie on the top of plants without harming them, lets in light, air and moisture, and does not cause rotting. Plants are less likely to suffer from the wind damage that plastic film can cause. Unlike plastic sheeting, fleece 'breathes', so can stay in place until the plants mature. Hold it in place by burying its edges in the soil, or anchoring them with bricks.

To make a fleece cloche, staple a piece of the material between two wooden laths. Place over a row of plants such as young cauliflowers to protect them from rabbits, pigeons, cabbage butterflies, and cabbage moth. Secure the laths with a brick in windy weather.

FORCING JARS

These accelerate growth so plants can be enjoyed earlier than normal, and are often made from terracotta. They provide warmth and protection and/or exclude light. Rhubarb, for example, is forced in tall, open-topped pots. The stems grow long and succulent as they reach towards the light.

RIGHT **Forcing jars**

CHAPTER 3

Choosing vegetable seed and plants

Deciding which vegetables you want to grow can be daunting, as the range of seed and plants available is increasing all the time. One way to begin is to eliminate the vegetables that can be bought easily and relatively inexpensively, and grow things like celeriac, scorzonera, seakale and asparagus which can be more expensive. Another option is to grow things that taste best when really fresh, like lettuce or sweetcorn. Flavour must, of course, come first, but remember that some vegetables are more suitable for freezing. Plan the next season's crops when the seed catalogues arrive in winter. Grow what your family enjoys, but grow a small quantity of a vegetable you have not tried before as well. Sow short rows of fast-maturing varieties at frequent intervals, so that you will be able to harvest a succession of vegetables that are in peak condition.

ABOVE **Carrots, peas and broad beans growing companionably together**

If you want or need only a small crop of a particular vegetable, it is best to buy plants. If this is not the case, growing vegetables from seed offers a greater choice. It is also cheaper, and lets you experiment with different varieties. A greenhouse is not essential, but it will provide a protected environment that will allow you to over-winter your plants and encourage tender seedlings into early growth.

Tailor what you grow to the space available, and try to estimate your yield accurately. If you grow more plants than you can use reasonably quickly or freeze and store, the rest may 'bolt', flower, then produce seed. If your plot is small, consider dwarf varieties and container-grown crops. Plants such as loose-leaf lettuce and sprouting broccoli that regenerate after cutting are useful for small plots.

With such a wide choice of vegetables, it is important to understand the prevailing conditions in your garden and choose varieties to suit them. Never try to grow anything that will not like the conditions in your garden. Check the source of plants to avoid diseases such as club-root on brassicas and white rot on onions or leeks.

Perennial vegetables such as rhubarb, asparagus and globe artichokes, are bought as plants rather than seed. Buy only virus-free or tested plants, and choose virus-free seed potatoes. It is often more convenient to buy plants such as cucumbers, sweet peppers, aubergines, celery and celeriac and tomatoes from garden centres or nurseries.

ABOVE **Planting radish 'Jaba' on surface of wet compost**

RIGHT **Runner beans growing happily in a quiet corner**

BUYING SEED

Seed should be as fresh as possible to ensure that it will germinate and sprout. Always buy good quality seed from a reputable source, preferably disease-resistant. Choose seed that has been packed in humidity-controlled, airtight, watertight, heat- and cold-resistant sealed packets. It is worth considering a mail-order catalogue, as seed stored in damp conditions or exposed to too much heat may lose its viability or ability to germinate. In most countries, seed quality is controlled by legislation, so one grower's products will be much the same as another. Sow as soon as possible after opening as it will deteriorate once exposed to the air.

Vegetables grown organically under the right conditions and at the right time will be better able to fight off pests and diseases. Attack can also be prevented by growing plants bred for resistance. Plant breeders cross-cultivate plants with their wild relatives to produce varieties that are more resistant to common problems. The brassicas, for example, are vulnerable to attack from many pests and diseases, and because they are an important commercial crop, several resistant varieties are available. Unfortunately flavour, texture or cropping may suffer. Crops bred for size and succulence, however, have gradually become more attractive to pests and diseases because the genes that convey resistance have been lost.

Organically-grown seed usually resists disease better, and most catalogues now include some. Plants that produce 'organic' seed must be grown on established organic land and harvested, cleaned and stored without the use of chemicals. Organic seed is now available for most vegetables, though not always in the varieties you are looking for.

ABOVE **Pumpkins need a long, hot summer to ripen fully**

ABOVE **Chitted sweetcorn F1 'Sunrise' seed**

There is a huge choice of seed available and it can sometimes be difficult to know what to choose. The following guide may help you to decide what to use.

OPEN-POLLINATED SEED
These are non-hybrid traditional varieties that reproduce true to type. They have been grown and selected over a long time for their characteristics, are hardier and have a better flavour and more flexibility than their hybrid counterparts. Most varieties in seed catalogues are of this type.

VACUUM-PACKED SEED
This is packed into vacuum-sealed foil sachets, and maintains its viability longer than seed packed loose in paper envelopes.

CHITTED OR PRE-GERMINATED SEED
This is germinated by the grower and dispatched in waterproof sachets. Each seed must be planted carefully and without delay in a pot or seed tray. It is a good way to buy seed where germination is unreliable, or requires temperatures that are difficult to maintain without a propagator.

PELLETED SEED
These are individually coated with clay or other material to form a smooth ball. They cost more, but fewer are required. They can be handled separately and are more easily spaced in containers or open ground. Pelleting is useful for tiny seeds as you can space-sow them at the correct distance and negate the need for thinning. Pelleted seeds must be watered thoroughly after sowing to ensure that the moisture needed for germination will penetrate the seed coat as quickly as possible. If the seed is kept too dry or too wet, germination will be poor. Pelleted seeds are normally only available for F1 and F2 hybrids.

F1 HYBRID
This is the result of genetic breeding, but it is sometimes sterile and will not germinate. It is also more expensive, because of the cost of breeding programmes. Hybrid seeds are genetically identical, so the whole crop will have uniform characteristics of size, height, form, flavour and colour. They also give higher yields, are more disease-resistant, and usually mature earlier. They are ideal for producing uniformly-maturing crops for freezing. Never save the seed from F1 hybrids as it will not produce plants that are true to type. This means that you will have to buy your seed every year if you want the same results.

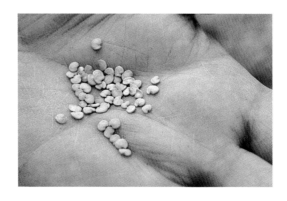

RIGHT **Aubergine 'Long Tom' seeds**

ABOVE **Pak choi seedlings in a compartmentalised seed tray**

COLLECTING YOUR OWN SEED

Vegetable seeds can be saved to sow the following spring. Collect seeds from vegetables such as runner and French beans, peas and onions in autumn. Runner and French beans are particularly good as they are expensive to buy, but easy to collect and usually breed true. Choose one or two of your best plants early in the season and label 'leave for seed collection' to remind you not to pull them up. Let the pods on these plants develop and ripen fully. Collect seed when it rattles in its pod or flowers, on a sunny day, shaking it free of its casing. Leave onion plants to flower on their own to avoid cross-pollination with inferior plants. Gather the ripe onion seed carefully as it is easily scattered, or tie a paper bag over the seed heads to catch the seeds as they fall. Label envelopes with the name of the vegetable and date of collection, and store in a cool, dry, dark place until spring. Saved seed can also be stored in small plastic containers such as old film cases.

BELOW **Tray of 'Tiny Tim' tomato plants**

STORING SURPLUS SEED

Opened seed packets, apart from pelleted seed, can be closed tightly and placed in a screw-topped jar. Label and date each packet and store the jar in a cool, dry, dark place. If you are unsure of the viability of left-over seed, sow a few between two pieces of damp absorbent paper and put them in a warm place. If they have not sprouted in a couple of weeks, discard the seed.

BUYING PLANTS

If you only need two or three plants for a container, it makes sense to buy young plants. Garden centres generally offer a good range, and more unusual varieties can be ordered from a seed catalogue. Lettuces, corn and cabbages are usually sold in strips of about 12 plants, while aubergines, sweet peppers, courgettes, cucumbers, marrows and tomatoes are sold singly in pots. Garden centres display vegetable plants from early spring, but many cannot be planted out until later. If you buy them early, you will need to keep them frost-free for several weeks, and will probably need to pot them on at least once to prevent a check in their growth. If you wait until later in the season, the plants you want may be sold out or of inferior quality. Whenever you buy, make sure you buy only top-quality plants.

ABOVE **Recycled camera film containers are ideal for storing collected seed**

CHOOSING VEGETABLE PLANTS

1 Look for robust plants with healthy green foliage. Straggly or 'leggy' plants have been deprived of light; those with discoloured foliage are usually lacking in nutrients or have been exposed to frost.

2 Buy plants that have just come into the store. Plants grown in small amounts of compost over a period of time soon dry out.

3 Do not buy bare-rooted brassicas as they could introduce club root into your soil.

4 Do not buy calabrese or cauliflower. Both of these can suffer a check to growth and 'bolt'.

LEFT **Planting soaked 'Boltardy' beetroot seeds in a prepared drill**

SOWING SEED

Do not be tempted to sow too early or you may end up with spindly, pale seedlings that will never make good plants. Make a list of what you have and when you need to sow. This will enable you to group plants, plan when to sow them, and help you to manage your greenhouse space efficiently.

MULTIPLE SOWING

This is the best way to produce some of your early crops. Sow groups of seeds in polystyrene trays or plastic cells and leave in a warm place. When the seedlings germinate, move them to a cooler place until they are large enough to plant out under cloches. Deep beds are ideal for many multiple sown crops, including leeks, onions, turnips, carrots and beetroot.

SUCCESSIONAL SOWING

The aim of the vegetable gardener is to produce a year-round supply of fresh vegetables, supplemented by home-frozen ones if necessary. One way to do this is to make several sowings at regular intervals. Try successive sowings of vegetables such as turnips, spinach, radish, lettuce, salad onions, kohl rabi and beetroot.

ABOVE **Chitted organic soya beans**

SPACE SOWING

Put two or three large or pelleted seeds in a newly watered seed drill at the recommended planting distance. Cover and label. Thin the seedlings to one seedling per station, discarding the weaker ones.

FLUID SOWING

Mix the seeds with fungicide-free wallpaper paste and place the mixture in a plastic bag. Cut off one corner of the bag and squirt along the length of a prepared drill.

SOWING FINE SEED

Mix seed that is fine and difficult to handle with a small quantity of silver sand. Sprinkle pinches of the sand/seed mix evenly along the prepared row. Very fine seed will need a very shallow covering or no covering at all.

CHITTING

Line a tray with moist kitchen paper and sprinkle with seeds. Cover the container and keep in a warm place (70°F /21°C) until they germinate.

BROADCASTING

Rake the soil to a fine tilth and scatter seed over it as evenly as possible, by hand or from the packet. Rake lightly afterwards to cover seeds.

LEFT **Planting squash 'Butternut Sprinter'**

ABOVE **Chitting organic soya beans between two layers of damp kitchen paper**

CUT-AND-COME-AGAIN SEEDLING CROPS

This is a productive way to use a small area of ground. Crops are harvested at their seedling stage and resprout to produce a second and third crop. Leafy or salad vegetables including lettuce, cress, chicory, curly endive, mustard, kale, and oriental greens such as pak choi, can all be grown in this way. They are ideal for sowing between slower-maturing vegetables.

SEED BEDS

A well-made seedbed will produce good seedlings that can be transplanted, such as leeks, lettuce and summer and winter brassicas. Normal organic methods of soil preparation (see page 71) will produce a good workable soil structure. After the initial digging in late autumn/winter, choose a fine day in early spring and fork over the soil, breaking down any large clods of earth. Rake over the seedbed, remove any large stones or debris, and sprinkle fertilizer over the top. Trample the soil down well with your feet to provide a firm seedbed. Finally, rake the soil into a fine tilth, standing on a board if you cannot reach it from a path. Use a garden line for guidance and a measuring stick for larger seeds, so the rows are straight and the seeds correctly spaced.

Transplant the seedlings to their permanent bed when they are about 2in (5cm) tall, usually 5–7 weeks after sowing. Water the row of seedlings the day before lifting them. Lift carefully, retaining as much soil as possible. Discard plants with bent stems and those without growing points. Keep the roots covered so that they do not dry out. Mark out the planting row with pegs and string to keep them straight. Check the planting distances and make holes with a dibber. Fill any dry holes with water and plant once they have drained. Check the required planting depth. Always use a line when planting out and a yardstick to check spacing in the row. Firm planting is essential, so firm them in with your fingers and water the base of each one as soon as the row has been planted. If the weather is warm, cover your plants with newspaper and water the soil frequently so it does not dry out before they are established.

OUTDOOR SOWING

The best seeds to sow outdoors are those of hardy crops like beans and peas, those which germinate easily, such as beetroot, and those which dislike being transplanted, like endive. Check the seed packets for sowing times. Seeds can be sown up to a month earlier if you use cloches. Position the cloches two weeks before sowing to warm up the soil. If you have light, well-drained soil in a sheltered spot, try sowing broad beans or peas for very early crops.

INTERCROPPING

Different vegetables can be combined in a single bed to give maximum yield. Fast-growing crops such as radishes and lettuces can be planted at the same time as slower-growing crops like parsnips and corn. Fast-growing crops reach maturity and can be harvested before the slow-growing ones need the space to develop. Try planting alternate rows of the selected crops.

ABOVE **Making a drill with a draw hoe and garden line**

SEED DRILLS

Make a shallow, V-shaped seed drill at the recommended depth, using a draw hoe and a straight garden line as a guide. Water the length of the drill. Sow the seed thinly, as seedlings that have to compete for light are likely to be straggly. Sown thinly, the seedlings will be more resistant to disease and need less thinning. Use the hoe to draw the dry soil back over the drill, covering the seeds. Firm by pressing down with the back of the hoe. Label the row.

Thin out the seedlings in stages. Remove every other plant to start with, then thin again a week or so later, following the instructions on the seed packet. It is easier to thin seedlings if you water first. After thinning, water again to settle the soil back around the roots.

LEFT **Beetroot is ideal for outdoor sowing**

DEEP BEDS

If space is limited, sowing seed in deep beds will allow vegetables to be grown closer together and increase their yields. Dig the soil deeply and work in plenty of organic matter. This raises the ground, which improves drainage. The extra soil depth also promotes strong root growth. After digging, all work must be done from the side of the bed, because if the soil is trodden on it will become compacted. To keep the ground in good condition, mulch each spring with organic matter.

SOWING UNDER GLASS

Place a sheet of glass over the tray or pot containing the newly-sown seeds and cover with a sheet of brown paper. Keep the tray at a temperature of 60–70°F (16–21°C). Wipe the glass daily to remove any condensation. When the seedlings emerge, remove the brown paper and prop up the sheet of glass. Remove the glass after a few days and move the tray or pot close to the light. Keep the compost moist. As soon as the first set of true leaves have opened, prick the seedlings out into trays or small pots, ½in (12mm) apart. Keep the trays or pots in the

ABOVE **Corn salad seedlings**

shade for one or two days. When the seedlings have recovered, harden them off by moving them to a cool room and increasing ventilation. Move the trays or pots outside during daylight and bring them inside at night. About a week before planting, leave them out all the time.

BELOW **Seedtrays of healthy seedlings ready for planting**

INDOOR SOWING

For indoor sowing, you will need seed trays, pots or cell trays. Trays are fine if you have a lot of seeds, but it is often difficult to give them the space they need in order to germinate. Transplant before they become overcrowded.

Small pots are ideal for large seeds like cucumbers and marrows. Cell trays are useful as individual seeds can be sown in each cell, and seedlings can grow quite large before you need to move them on. You will also need a large tray to hold water. Placing pots or cells in a large tray so they soak up the right amount of water gradually is much better than using a watering can. A dibber is useful for making holes to sow larger seeds. A seedling fork is great for lifting seedlings at transplanting time. Use a flat board to firm or level off the compost. but make sure it will fit in the tray.

ABOVE **Broad beans**

Choose a loam-based compost or a proprietary peat or peat-free seed/cuttings compost that is non-organic but low in nutrients. Rich compost can prevent seed germination, and multi-purpose composts will have a little more nutrient. Label your trays and pots with the name of the vegetable and the date the seeds were sown. A propagator is useful, but not vital.

METHOD

1 Fill the tray or pot with compost and remove any excess.

2 Firm the compost with the flat board.

3 Sow the seeds thinly in the tray to avoid fatal fungal infections, or sow larger seeds singly in a small pot.

4 Cover the seed lightly with more compost if necessary (check packet).

5 Place the tray or pot in a large tray of water and let the compost soak it up. When it has darkened, remove the seed tray or pot, drain, and label. Place in a propagator, cover trays or pots with clear film, or place in plastic bags (to stop them drying out). Place on a sunny windowsill or in the airing cupboard.

6 When the seedlings appear, give them light and remove any ailing or dead ones.

7 When the seedlings have developed their first true leaves, prick them out. Make sure the compost is moist and always hold seedlings by their seed leaves – the first leaves that appear after germination and the lowest on the stem. Avoid touching the true leaves and never handle the stem; a crushed seedling will never recover.

8 Transplant the seedlings.

HOT BEDS

These are manure-filled sunken beds that allow crops to be started off far earlier than when grown in open ground. Many organic gardeners use manure for its nutritional and soil-improving properties.

Hot beds were traditionally used on large estates run by armies of gardeners, but it is easy to adapt the design for your own garden. In the past, they were permanent structures, made in a frame of bricks and mortar. Today's gardeners will find it far easier to dig out a large pit. A hot bed made from fresh manure will usually last for several months. The manure generates the warmth needed to start off the crops early.

BELOW **Courgette 'Gold Rush' seedlings showing how the whole seed pushes out of the compost**

METHOD

1 Dig a pit at least 18in (45cm) deep and wide. If your soil is heavy, spike the bottom of the pit after digging to loosen the soil and allow water to drain away.

2 Place fresh manure in the pit, breaking up large clumps with a fork. You will need a considerable quantity, but it can be bulked out with straw or organic compost. Keep moist.

3 Water well, and cover with a layer of soil 4–5in (10–12.5cm) deep.

4 Allow the soil to settle for a few days, adding more if necessary. Heat will be produced as the organic matter decomposes.

5 Cover the bed with a cloche or polythene to retain the heat ready for planting.

ABOVE **Baby kohl rabi 'Logo' seedlings**

COMPOST

Most composts are based on peat, sand and chemical fertilizers. Some are based on sterilized soil, although they may still have some peat in them. Organic versions may be similar, or based on composted or worm-produced waste material. Many conventional and most peat-free and organic composts have proved inferior to the best peat-based or loam-based commercial composts. If you prefer peat-free compost, there are many brands available. You may also wish to make your own organic compost, but it is probably best to buy a popular brand from a reputable supplier to get your seeds off to a good start.

LEFT **Broad beans 'The Sutton'**

MAKING DEGRADABLE POTS

The organic gardener always uses natural products rather than ozone-damaging ones. He or she also recycles household waste such as newspapers – paper and cardboard make up 33 per cent of what we throw away – using them as a mulch or shredding them for the compost heap. Newspapers can also be used to make bio-degradable pots for raising seeds and cuttings in the greenhouse.

If you want a bigger diameter for larger seeds such as runner beans, shape the pots round a wine bottle instead of a rolling pin.

YOU WILL NEED:
2 sheets of newspaper per pot
Glue
Rolling pin
Scissors

1 Wrap the newspaper around the rolling pin and glue the edges together to form a paper cylinder.

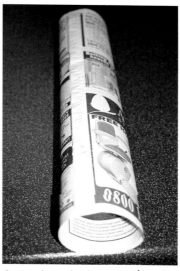

3 Cut the cylinder into 4½in (12cm) lengths (3 pots per cylinder).

2 Slide the cylinder off the rolling pin and allow the glue to dry.

4 Stand the pots in a seed tray and fill with coir compost.

SPROUTED SEEDS

It is easy to produce organically grown, crunchy sprouts that are full of vitamins. The sprouts can be eaten raw or stir-fried using a little oil. Sprout beans, peas or whole pulses and keep them in dark, damp conditions for several days, depending on what you are sprouting. Mung beans will produce two cups of sprouts in 3–4 days. They must be rinsed 2–3 times a day while they are growing to remove the toxins that are produced.

METHOD

1 Place the beans in a wide-necked jar. Their volume will increase about six times, so do not use too many. Cover with a piece of muslin and secure with an elastic band. Leave in a warm, dark place, preferably at a temperature of around 68°F (20°C). Brown paper tied around the jar will also exclude light.

2 Run fresh water into the jar through the muslin 2–3 times a day. Swill it round to wash the beans, then pour out the water. Leave the jar at an angle for a short time to ensure all the liquid drains away.

3 When the bean sprouts are ready to eat, turn them out of the jar or colander into a bowl of cold water. Rinse them well to wash off the outer seed coats. Drain, and use as required. They will keep for several days in the bottom of a refrigerator.

YOU WILL NEED

Glass jar
Organic sprouting mix
Muslin
Elastic band

ABOVE **Put some organic sprouting mix into a jam jar**

ABOVE **Place a piece of muslin over the jar and secure it with an elastic band**

ABOVE **Mung beans beginning to sprout**

ABOVE **Jars of sprouting beans on the windowsill**

ALTERNATIVE GROWING METHOD

Line a colander with two pieces of towelling, soaked in cold water. Place over a bowl so that any surplus drains away. Place the beans on the towelling. Rinse the beans 2–3 times a day with fresh water, taking care not to disturb the beans or towelling.

RIGHT **Sprouted aduki beans ready for use**

CHAPTER 4

Growing vegetables

Organic gardeners strive to achieve a balance in their gardens so they do not need chemicals to control pests and diseases. For vegetables to grow successfully, the soil must be rich and fertile. To grow organic vegetables, the plot is cropped intensively. Different crops take different nutrients from the soil, and these must be replaced continually to avoid exhausting it. There are many different ways to do this without the use of chemicals. Careful plot management produces the best returns and the heaviest crops. If you grow just one kind of crop year after year, it can exhaust the soil of the nutrients it requires, but varying the crops you grow can allow nutrients to be replenished. Crop rotation helps to maintain soil fertility, as well as helping to prevent some pests and diseases from building up to damaging proportions. Soil fertility also encourages worms and beneficial microbes, leading to better results.

ABOVE **Flowers and vegetables fill the border**

CROP ROTATION

For most gardens, rotating vegetables from strip to strip over a three-year period is ideal. Group crops with similar needs and move them round in a regular order to make better use of resources. Alternating shallow and deep-rooting vegetables improves the soil structure and can also help weed control. Leave a section for crops such as rhubarb, globe artichokes (grown as perennials or annuals), Jerusalem artichokes, asparagus and seakale that will not be included in the rotation plan. In small gardens, these permanent crops can also be grown in the ornamental or flower border. Runner beans grown at the end of the plot form an attractive screen and are easier to harvest. Onions are usually grouped with the legumes.

KEEPING RECORDS

Make a chart and draw in a column for each month of the year. Add the vegetables from your list, filling in the months in which each will be in the ground. Allow for plants that will be transplanted, crops that are sown once a year, and crops that need successional sowings.

To plan the rotation groups, divide a sheet of paper into four sections. In sections 1–3, note the most important crop, then choose a crop to follow or precede it. Each section will probably bear only two crops per year, for example: sprouting broccoli/dwarf French beans. Use section 4 for 'permanent' vegetables.

It is also a good idea to keep a crop diary with dates of planting, transplanting, harvesting, successes and failures.

BASIC CROP-ROTATION PLAN

Year 1
Group 1 – Legumes
Group 2 – Brassicas
Group 3 – Root crops

Year 2
Group 2 – Brassicas
Group 3 – Root crops
Group 1 – Legumes

Year 3
Group 3 – Root crops
Group 1 – Legumes
Group 2 – Brassicas

Group 1: Legumes and other crops
Before sowing, dig the soil well and add manure or compost.
Suitable crops: peas, beans, celery, leeks, lettuce, onions

Group 2: Brassicas
About two weeks before sowing or planting, rake in general-purpose fertilizer and add lime, unless you are sure the soil is alkaline.
Suitable crops: Brussels sprouts, cabbage, cauliflower, swede, sprouting broccoli, turnip, radish

Group 3: Root crops
About two weeks before sowing or planting, rake in a general-purpose fertilizer. Do not add manure or lime.
Suitable crops: beetroot, carrot, parsnip, potatoes, tomatoes

Group 4: Permanent crops (non-rotation)
To keep the soil rich and fertile, replenish essential nutrients and major plant foods regularly with manure and fertiliser.
Suitable crops: rhubarb, globe artichokes, Jerusalem artichokes, asparagus, seakale

PESTS AND DISEASES

Overcrowded, weak, straggly, stressed plants are more susceptible to disease and pest infestation. The best defence is to grow them in well-prepared soil with added organic matter and the right amount of nutrients and water. Plants that make soft growth are vulnerable to attack by aphids, which suck the sap from the leaves and shoots causing leaf curling and distortion, stunted growth and a black, sooty mould. These insects spread viral diseases from one plant to another, and can cause considerable damage. To control pests, use only derris, pyrethrum and insecticidal soap, all of which have no long-term damaging effects.

Plants need space so light and air can circulate. Plant at the right time, so they are established before there is any danger of pest infestation or disease. Growing different types of vegetables together can help, as can sowing flowers and herbs among or near them. The cottage garden tradition of mixing vegetables, herbs and flowers is also practical, as the different scents confuse pests.

ABOVE **Black fly on globe artichoke**

SLUGS AND OTHER PESTS

One way to deal with slugs is to go out at night armed with a torch and a bucket of soapy water. But there are other ways. Slugs and snails will hide under the skin of half a grapefruit or melon that is left on the ground. A shady canopy of herbs will encourage ground beetles, which have an enormous appetite for slugs. Make an effective trap by sinking a small dish into the ground. Half-fill with milk or beer to attract slugs, which will fall in and drown. Keep the rim about 1in (2.5cm) above ground level to avoid trapping ground beetles. Pick off caterpillars, snails and aphids by hand. Stick to a rigid hygiene regime: pests and diseases breed in rubbish heaps, rotting leaves and debris, decaying crops and weeds, dirty pots and seed trays, and soil brought into the greenhouse.

ABOVE **Slugs are a nuisance and cause damage to many different types of vegetable**

SOIL FERTILITY

Rich, fertile soil is required for successful gardening. All soil contains reserves of plant foods but these nutrients are not replenished naturally until plants die and rot down. Continuous cultivation and harvesting upsets the balance, causing a shortage of nutrients so plants fail to thrive. Leaching by rain also depletes essential plant foods. To maintain and increase soil fertility, major plant foods and trace elements must be returned at regular intervals in the form of manure and fertilizers. Artificial fertilizers are unnecessary; organic ones are simple to use, safe and natural, and usually last far longer than their chemical counterparts.

Soil constituents most likely to be in short supply are nitrogen, phosphate and potash. Nitrogen is known as the leaf maker, as vegetables grown for their leaves are most in need of nitrogen. Phosphate is the root maker, as root vegetables need large amounts for healthy growth. Potash is essential for flowers and fruit.

All plants require micronutrients for healthy growth, though applying large quantities can damage them. These include calcium for cell production; magnesium for the production of chlorophyll, the green colour in plants that absorbs sunlight, and sulphur which boosts the plant's immunity and is used in photosynthesis. Other micronutrients required in minute amounts are boron, chlorine, copper, iron, manganese, molybdenum, nickel and zinc.

SOIL SICKNESS

If you grow the same crop on the same site during successive years, yields often start to fall. This is caused by the gradual build-up of soil pests or soil-borne diseases and is known as soil sickness. As these pests only attack closely related 'family' groups, cultivating a different 'family' stops them from building up into damaging numbers.

ABOVE **Sweetcorn and nasturtiums in the flower border**

SOIL LAYERS

To achieve the best from your soil, it is necessary to recognize its two main layers. Topsoil is the fertile upper layer that contains beneficial bacteria and organic matter. In chalk soil, the topsoil layer can be as shallow as 2in (5cm), while on well-cultivated ground it can be up to 24in (60cm) deep. Usually it is around 12in (30cm) deep. When digging, never bury topsoil under subsoil; bag it for future use. Subsoil lacks organic matter and bacteria and is usually lighter in colour. Never dig it up to cover topsoil.

SOIL TYPES

Some plants are far more fussy than others in their requirements, so it is vital to determine your soil type. The ideal soil is a mixture of sand and clay with a large amount of humus. It is dark and rich in colour with a crumbly, medium-loam texture, well-drained subsoil, sufficient lime to counteract soil sourness, a substantial amount of humus and sufficient plant foods for maximum growth. The structure of the subsoil affects the drainage of the topsoil.

Clay soil sticks together in a lump or bakes hard in the sun with deep cracks. It takes a long time to warm up in spring, but is normally well supplied with plant foods and can support a variety of plants. It can be turned into workable, fertile soil by adding plenty of bulky organic matter, and improving drainage.

Sandy soil is light, easy to work, warms up quickly in spring, and can be cultivated earlier than most soils. It is gritty and does not lump together because it is free-draining. It is poor in nutrients, which are easily lost, and large amounts of organic matter and extra fertilizer should be added.

Chalky, pale, free-draining soils, are similar to sandy ones, but are always alkaline: they contain a great deal of lime. Alkaline soils can be deficient in manganese and iron, which can

ABOVE **Heavy clay soil**

cause yellowing leaves and stunted growth. The topsoil is usually shallow, so it is unsuitable for plants with deep roots. Water and nutrients need to be retained by adding organic material, which will also help to make the soil more acid. If soil is orange-yellow in colour, hard and cracked, it could be subsoil from which the topsoil has been removed. Subsoil is lighter in colour than topsoil because it contains no humus and is largely without nutrients. Your only choice may be to have new topsoil delivered.

SOIL WARMING

Plants can grow only if their roots have the right conditions. Most require a soil temperature of around 45°F (7°C) to develop and grow quickly. Unfortunately, many vegetables are ready to be transplanted when the soil temperature is still too low. To overcome this, cover the planting area with black plastic. This will warm up the soil by absorbing and trapping the sun's heat and raising the temperature of the upper layers of the soil, making early planting possible. The area can also be covered with cloches two weeks before planting.

LEFT **Workable loamy soil**

IMPROVING SOIL STRUCTURE

Spread bulky organic matter over the surface of the soil in autumn or early winter, at a rate of 10lb/sq yd (4.5kg/sq m). If your soil is starved of organic material, spread over the whole area, otherwise, just manure the area to be used for growing legumes and other crops (Group 1). Fork the layer of humus into the surface of the soil before you start digging. This will improve crumb structure and greatly increase the nutrient and water-holding capacity.

The acidity of your plot will be increased both by heavy cropping and by the addition of humus and fertilizer. When following a crop rotation plan, lime only the area of soil on which you intend to grow brassicas (Group 2), in the year you intend to grow them. Never lime at random, and test your soil to work out how much to apply. Use ground limestone rather than hydrated lime.

Decide whether your plot is ready to be forked over by walking its length and breadth wearing boots. If the soil sticks to them, it is still too wet and unworkable. If not, it is ready.

1 Turn over the surface with a fork, breaking down the clods of earth left from the autumn/early winter digging. Remove deep-rooted perennial weeds such as docks or nettles.

2 Break down the surface further until it forms a crumbly texture.

3 Apply a dressing of fertilizer, working it into the top few inches/centimetres of soil.

4 Level the seedbed by raking over in one direction and again at right angles, removing large stones and annual weeds as you go. If the area is too wide to reach from a path, stand on a board so you do not compact the soil and damage its structure.

SOIL ACIDITY

This is an important factor, and is dependent on how much calcium the soil contains. The acidity or alkalinity of soil is measured on the pH scale from 1–14. A reading of pH7 indicates a neutral soil; above pH7 the soil is alkaline and below it is acid. Carry out a pH test every year using a simple kit from a garden centre or nursery. Most vegetables grow best in slightly acid soil with a reading of around pH6.5. Brassicas should be planted in slightly alkaline soils with a reading of around pH7.5. If your own soil has a reading below pH6, add lime during the winter.

ABOVE **A soil testing kit showing a pH reading of 6.5, which denotes a slightly acid soil. Full instructions will be included with each kit**

COMPANION PLANTING

Certain plants seem to have beneficial effects on other kinds of plant grown nearby. Plants used in this way are known as companion plants, and are especially useful in the vegetable garden. Suitable companion plants are listed for each vegetable included in the A–Z Directory.

Companion plants may exude a scent that attracts insects which will pollinate other plants, or repel insects that damage them. They may condition or feed the soil, or release nitrogen for use by other plants. They may help to create the right microclimate for another plant. Good companion plants include herbs and nectar- and pollen-rich flowers. A small patch of flowering wild flowers will attract butterflies and bees. Marigolds, nasturtiums, poppies and convolvulus will minimize aphids by attracting insects such as hoverflies that prey upon them. Dead nettles provide cover for predators like frogs and beetles, which eat insects.

ABOVE **French marigolds attract beneficial insects**

ORGANIC FERTILIZERS

Organic fertilizers supply plants with the nutrients they need over a period of time, and last far longer in the soil than chemical ones. They are ecologically sound and environmentally safe. They do not harm the soil and, applied regularly, benefit the crops grown in it and the wildlife that live in it. They are of either animal or vegetable origin and are available in the form of powders, ground manure or pellets, which are the easiest to use. Apply according to the instructions on the packet.

BONEMEAL

Bonemel (30 per cent phosphates, 1.5 per cent nitrogen) is a favourite garden fertilizer and a good source of phosphate. The phosphate is released slowly, aiding seed germination, stimulating root and pod growth, and promoting the early ripening of fruits and roots. It is often used as a dressing for seedbeds as the ground bones break down slowly to release phosphate that is useful for root crops. Apply at the rate of 2–4oz per sq yd (50–100g per sq m). Always buy it steam-treated, as raw bone meal may contain anthrax. Wear gloves when applying.

BLOOD, FISH AND BONE

This useful, balanced general fertilizer is a mixture of dried blood, fish meal and ground bones. It releases nitrogen quickly, and phosphate more slowly. It can be used as a pre-planting dressing and as a compost activator.

SEAWEED MEAL

This is a useful multi-purpose fertilizer made from dried and ground seaweed. It supplies both trace elements and essential nutrients, and is also an excellent activator for the compost heap. Applied to the soil at the rate of 3oz per sq yd (75g per sq m) it is a good source of potash.

PELLETED POULTRY MANURE

This useful, fast-acting, general garden fertilizer is easy to apply and contains various nutrients including nitrogen. It can be used as a top-dressing for leafy plants such as kale, and as a compost activator. It has a strong smell.

COMFREY AND NETTLES

Rot down comfrey and nettle leaves in a bucket of water. The resulting liquid can be diluted to make a great fertilizer for most plants.

DRIED BLOOD

Dried blood (12–13 per cent nitrogen) is a fast-acting fertilizer that is particularly beneficial to leafy brassicas. Work into the soil when growth is active, or mix with water and apply around the roots of the plants. Apply at the rate of 1–2oz per sq yd (25–50g per sq m). Water in well after each application.

HOOF AND HORN

This is made from the ground, sterilized hooves and horns of cattle. It is a valuable source of nitrogen and is broken down by the bacteria in the soil over a long period, ensuring a steady supply of the element to the plants. It takes a long time to release nitrogen, so should be worked into the soil 2–3 weeks before planting.

WOOD ASH

This is the main organic supply of potash, and is quick-acting when applied to growing plants. Potash counteracts soft growth, and helps to form storage material in potato tubers and onion bulbs. It also counterbalances the effect of excess nitrogen, and increases resistance to disease by helping plants to withstand frost and drought. It can make wet soils stickier, so apply in spring when the soil is dry and hoe in well.

MULCHES

A mulch is a layer of material that covers the soil. Mulching helps to keep the ground weed free, reduces the effects of summer drought, protects the soil from heavy rain and acts as an insulating blanket to protect young or delicate roots from extremes of temperature. In winter, a layer of mulch reduces the risk of soil freezing around the roots of plants, and in summer it provides protection from the scorching sun.

A mulch can be inorganic, for example plastic or polythene, or organic, such as well-rotted manure, which should be spread to a depth of at least 4in (10cm) to be effective. Stone mulches are ideal for areas where drainage is necessary. Spread a layer of gravel to a thickness of 1–2in (2.5–5cm).

Take care when mulching as it also encourages slugs, prevents light rain from reaching the soil and as organic mulches decay, they become an ideal place for weed seed germination.

ABOVE **Bark for mulching**

GREEN MANURING

This is a natural way of replenishing soil nutrients. A suitable crop is grown but, instead of harvesting, it is allowed to mature and is then dug into the ground. Green manuring provides organic matter, increases biological activity, and the roots of the crop break up the soil and improve drainage. An autumn sowing of green manure will protect the vegetable plot over the winter. When it is dug into the ground it will decay and release valuable nutrients. If you wish to improve an area of soil, try putting it down to green manure for 6–12 months. For the following crop, choose one that is not similar to the one you have just harvested.

METHOD:

1 Sow the seed as directed on the packet.
2 Let the plants grow.
3 Dig the plants into the soil.
4 Allow to decay for at least two weeks.
5 Sow or plant the plot with another crop.

NITROGEN FIXERS:

Alfalfa or lucerne (*Medicago sativa*) is a tall perennial. It must occupy land for a full season.
Red clover (*Trifolium pratense*) is low-growing and can be dug in when the land is needed.
Winter tare (*Vicia sativa*) produces large amounts of green matter. Dig in early spring.

PLANTS THAT DO NOT FIX NITROGEN

Phacelia (*Phacelia tanacetifolia*) is fast growing but does not withstand cold. Dig it in about 8 weeks after sowing.
Rye (*Secale cereale*) produces a useful amount of green material. Sow the perennial variety and dig it in during spring.
Mustard (*Sinapis alba*) is fast-growing, a good weed suppressor and produces plenty of green matter. Dig in before flowering. It is a member of the cabbage family, so it may harbour club-root.

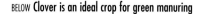

BELOW **Clover is an ideal crop for green manuring**

THE COMPOST HEAP

A good compost heap is the ideal way to return organic material to the soil. Compost is produced by the breakdown of organic material by micro-organisms (mostly bacteria and fungi) and should be brown and crumbly. It improves soil structure and fertility, provides plant foods and reduces the need for artificial fertilizers. Compost also increases worm activity and water-holding capacity.

Garden centres and DIY stores sell a variety of compost bins or containers, or you can make your own. Size will depend on space available, but the larger the receptacle the better the air circulation. Ideally, you should keep three compost containers: one to fill with current waste, one in the process of rotting down, and one that is ready for use. A wooden container that is divided into three sections is ideal (see diagram below).

MATERIALS FOR COMPOSTING

Vegetable waste
Grass clippings
Kitchen waste (not meat, fish or cooked food as they attract vermin)
Prunings (shred any woody ones first)
Pet manure and bedding (from vegetarian pets such as rabbits and guinea-pigs only)
Dead flowers
Fruit skins
Nettles
Used tea bags
Torn paper and cardboard
Shredded brassica stems

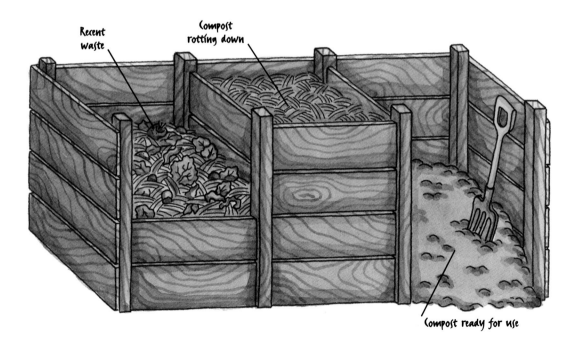

Recent waste

Compost rotting down

Compost ready for use

ABOVE **A three-section compost container**

THE COMPOSTING PROCESS

Soft, sappy material such as grass clippings will rot down first. These feed micro-organisms and increase heat to speed up the composting. The heap must also have air, nitrogen, lime, water, heat and bacteria. With the right balance, the compost can heat up to 140–158°F (60–70°C), which is hot enough to kill most weed seeds and some diseases. When the soft material has been used up, the micro-organisms start to work on the woody material. Shred woody material before adding it to the bin to increase the surface area available for the micro-organisms to work on and speed composting. Activity decreases and the bin cools down. If the bin is open at the bottom larger organisms like worms and beetles start to work. After a few months, the contents of the bin become dark and crumbly. The compost is ready to use when it has a fine texture and is virtually odourless.

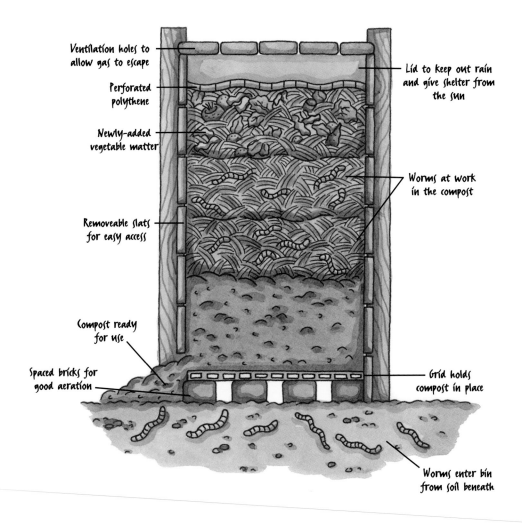

ABOVE **A compost bin showing the different layers**

76

METHOD

1 Stand the container/bin on a layer of spaced bricks to provide drainage and allow the air to reach the composting material from beneath.

2 Build up the heap in layers 12in (30cm) deep, taking care not to pack the layers too tightly. Spread/sprinkle organic manure or a nitrogenous fertilizer over every second layer. Add lime to each alternate layer.

3 Cover with a sheet of perforated polythene and a lid and leave to rot down.

USING A WORMERY

This is a self-contained unit in which special worms break down organic waste into rich, dark compost, a process known as vermiculture. It is a good alternative to a compost heap if you live in a townhouse or apartment and have only kitchen waste to compost. Wormeries are small and can be kept in a garage, shed or even indoors. The worms thrive on a diet of fruit and vegetable peelings, and will also eat cereal, coffee grounds, stale bread and tea bags. They chomp their way through material many times their own weight and process it, reducing its volume by up to 80 per cent. The result is a useful compost for plants, and a liquid that can be drained off and used as a plant food. Wormeries and the special worms to activate them are available from garden suppliers. Ordinary earthworms cannot be used because the conditions are too rich.

WARNING

Never put clippings from lawns recently treated with weedkillers, or chemically-treated weeds on a compost heap. Avoid anything that has been exposed to household or garden chemicals, and check for hard objects such as stones, bits of metal, plastic or glass.

RIGHT **Rich, home-produced compost produces excellent crops**

PREPARING YOUR PLOT

Good ground preparation is the secret of good crops. Digging corrects the structural damage caused by rain and heavy footsteps, which compresses the soil, damages the crumb structure and impairs drainage. Dig the soil in the vegetable garden every year, or every five or six years if the deep bed system is used.

You will be sowing in spring, so prepare your plot in late autumn or early winter. Remove any debris such as stones or pieces of wood, and cut down tall weeds and grass with a strimmer. Measure and mark it out into four sections, so you can follow a crop rotation plan. Use canes and twine or strong string to mark out the plot.

Dig the soil roughly, leaving it in fairly large lumps. This will allow winter frosts to break it up and improve its texture. It also introduces air, and encourages the biological activity that is necessary for soil fertility. In early spring the soil should be crumbly, workable and just moist.

Do not dig when the soil is very wet or the structure may be harmed. Avoid digging light soils; instead, spread layers of well-rotted organic material over it as a mulch. Allow the worms to incorporate the humus into the soil and improve its fertility. Young plants can then be grown through the mulch.

SINGLE DIGGING

Dig each area separately to the depth of one spit – the length of your spade's blade. Do not try to dig the whole area at once. Spread the digging over a few days to prevent any strain or injury. When you are digging, take care not to bring up any of the subsoil. Working from one side of the plot to the other, dig out a trench. Fork over the bottom of the trench as you work to break up the subsoil. Barrow the soil from the first trench to the far end of the plot, and leave it to fill the last trench you dig. Dig a second trench, and use the soil to fill in the first trench. As you turn the soil, fork in organic matter. Continue digging trenches to the end of each area. Use the soil from the third trench to fill the second trench and so on across the plots, keeping the soil as level as possible. Finish by filling the last trench with the soil from the first.

DOUBLE DIGGING

This is similar to single digging, but to twice the depth! Work from side to side of the plot as above, but this time digging to a depth of two spits and producing trenches about 18in (45cm) deep. Rake over and level the whole area. Double-digging encourages vegetables to form good root systems, and breaks up compacted soil that may have formed below the depth of normal digging. Dig soil that is not free draining to this depth every three–four years.

LEFT **Digging main crop of potatoes**

HARVESTING

Harvest crops at their peak and eat or freeze when they are really fresh. As soon as vegetables are picked, their vitamin levels start to drop. Water the evening before and pick very early the next day, or, if this is not possible, in the cool of the evening. Once harvested, keep them as cool as possible.

STORING PRODUCE

Most leafy crops can be stored in a refrigerator for up to a week. Some vegetables are suitable for freezing, including cauliflowers, runner beans, courgettes, Brussels sprouts, asparagus, and broad beans.

LEAVING PRODUCE IN THE GROUND

Some vegetables, including winter cabbages, leeks and Brussels sprouts can stand in the ground until they are needed. Root vegetables, such as swedes, turnips, parsnips and carrots can be left in well-drained soil until you are ready to harvest them.

STORING IN SAND

For easy access during the winter months, store root crops in boxes of sand in a cool, dry place such as a garage or shed. Remove foliage and lay the roots, the largest first, on a layer of moist sand. Cover with more sand.

ABOVE **Harvesting Chinese cabbage**

RIGHT **Newly-dug main crop of salad variety potatoes 'Ratte'**

LEFT **Flowers of the broad bean variety**
'The Sutton'

CHAPTER 5

A–Z plant directory

This directory does not claim to be an exhaustive list of vegetables, but it does include a good selection that will allow you to create an attractive and varied vegetable garden, wherever you may live. The individual vegetables are listed alphabetically with all the information you should need to get started. Popular varieties are listed after each vegetable. The final chapter lists some of the most popular companion plants.

NAMING OF PLANTS
If the description of the vegetable is all in italics, this is a naturally-occurring plant that has been discovered growing in habitat. For example, in *Daucus carota*, *Daucus* is the genus name and *carota* is the species name. This is a plant that was originally discovered growing in its native habitat, and is therefore a true species. Botanists may find slight variations, so if you see the terms f. or var. or subsp. they describe forms, varieties and subspecies that occur naturally.

If, however, you see a description like Carrot *Daucus carota* 'Amsterdam Forcing' it tells you that the plant is a cultivar, and that plant breeders and hybridizers have been selecting and crossing plants to produce a distinctive plant which they can name. If you see a description that has 'xxxx' after any name in this plant directory, you will know that it is a cultivar rather than a true species.

HARDINESS RATINGS
The information given is based on UK Royal Horticultural Society data, but is on the cautious side. If you are not prepared to take any chances, follow the hardiness rating to the letter. Otherwise, there is a great deal of leeway. Raised beds, good drainage, south-/south-west facing borders and planting against a house wall all give plants a better habitat – so be prepared to experiment. If you cannot bear the thought of losing your most valued plants, keep back-ups by taking cuttings or dividing the plants and growing spares.
Half-hardy: down to 32° F/0° C
Frost-hardy: down to 23° F/–5° C
Fully hardy: down to 5° F/–15° C
(FT) Frost tender

SAFETY WARNING:
Not all plant parts are safe to eat. Eat only those parts that you know are edible. If in doubt take expert advice.

Keep all fertilizers, sprays etc. in their properly labelled containers, and well out of the reach of children and pets. Read directions carefully and use according to the manufacturers' instructions.

NAME **ARTICHOKE – GLOBE**
CYNARA SCOLYMUS
FAMILY **COMPOSITAE**

Type: Hardy perennial

USDA zone: 8–9

Description: This massive, architectural plant looks rather like a giant thistle and may grow to 4ft (1.2m), with a 3ft (90cm) spread. It has arching, silvery leaves and green to deep purple heads, depending on variety. Heads that are not harvested will blossom into purple thistles.

Sowing and harvesting: Sow seed in spring for transplanting the following spring. Plant offsets (rooted suckers) about 9in (23cm) high in spring for harvesting during the summer of the second year onwards. Keep plants of different ages to ensure a succession of crops.

Where to grow: In light or loamy, fertile soil (pH6.5) in a sunny, sheltered position. The herbaceous border is ideal as the leaves are a perfect foil for brightly-coloured flowers.

How to grow: Sow thinly in 1in (2.5cm) deep drills, 12in (30cm) apart. Thin to 9in (23cm) and plant out the following spring. Seed gives variable results, so globe artichokes are usually grown from offsets from a nursery or taken from high-yield plants. Divide healthy plants in spring using two hand forks. Each division should have at least two shoots, good roots and a few leaves. Plant offsets 2–3ft (60–90cm) apart in rows 4ft (1.2m) apart. Bed size and shape will determine the number planted. Replace plants every 4–5 years.

Average yield: 10–12 heads per mature plant.

Maintenance: Water well until plants are established and in dry weather. Hoe regularly during summer and feed with a liquid fertilizer every two weeks. Cut down the stems in late autumn and cover the crowns with straw. Remove straw in spring. In the first year, a few small heads will start to form; cut them off immediately and add to your compost heap.

Harvesting and storing: Harvest in the summer of the second year onwards. Cut off the plump, fully-formed heads using a sharp knife, leaving a portion of stem attached. The scales should be soft and green. Primary harvesting encourages a second crop, which can be encouraged by giving the plants an organic liquid feed. Heads will stay fresh in a polythene bag in the refrigerator for up to a week.

Pests and diseases: Petal blight, fungus, aphids and slugs.

Other species and varieties:

'Green Globe' (organic) has traditional large green heads.

'Vert de Lyon' can be bought as offsets from garden centres.

Companion plants: Petunias, nasturtiums and marigolds.

ABOVE **The head of a mature globe artichoke**

NAME **ARTICHOKE – JERUSALEM**
HELIANTHUS TUBEROSUS
FAMILY **COMPOSITAE**

Type: Hardy perennial

USDA zone: All zones

Description: Jerusalem artichokes are grown for their tubers. They grow rapidly and can reach 10ft (3m) or more. The tubers are about 2–4in (5–10cm) long and look a bit like knobbly potatoes. If they are allowed, they will produce attractive, terminal yellow flowers like small sunflowers.

Sowing and harvesting: Plant tubers in late winter/early spring for harvesting from mid-autumn throughout the winter.

Where to grow: Jerusalem artichokes will tolerate most soils and are useful for breaking up heavy soil. They require medium nitrogen levels and do not like soil that is very acid or subject to prolonged waterlogging in winter. They make an excellent windbreak or fast-growing screen.

How to grow: Plant tubers in drills 4–6in (10–15cm) deep and 12in (30cm) apart with the main bud facing upwards. Cover with soil, taking care not to dislodge the tubers.

Average yield: 3–5lb (1.35–2.3kg) per plant.

Maintenance: When the plants are about 12in (30cm) high, earth up the base of the stems. Water in dry weather, and remove flower heads throughout the summer. Stake the stems on exposed sites, and cut them down to about 12in (30cm) in autumn.

Harvesting and storing: Lift the tubers as required, taking care not to damage the roots. They will stay fresh for up to two weeks in a polythene bag in the refrigerator, but keep best in the ground. A few tubers can be saved to replant the following year, but remove all small tubers after harvesting as they are invasive.

Pests and diseases: Slugs, sclerotinia rot.

Other species and varieties:

'Boston Red' is a knobbly variety that has rose-red skin.

'Fuseau' is a smoother, newer variety that is easier to use than the older varieties.

Companion plants: Petunias, pot marigolds, nasturtiums.

ABOVE **Chokes forming on a second year artichoke**

NAME **ASPARAGUS**
ASPARAGUS OFFICINALIS
FAMILY **LILIACEAE**

Type: Hardy perennial

USDA zone: 3 and above

Description: Asparagus is grown for its young shoots, which are cut as succulent spears. It is decorative, with feathery green foliage that appears in summer. Plants may be female (berry bearing) or male, which are more productive.

Crowns: 'Grolim F1' has thick spears with tightly-closed heads.

'Backlim F1' is an all-male variety with a good yield of thick, smooth spears. It can be grown as green or white asparagus.

Sowing and harvesting: Asparagus can be raised from seed sown in late winter, but the plants must not be cropped until they are three years old. Crowns, usually a year old, can be bought and planted in spring. Cut spears sparingly in the second year, then regularly in the third year. Harvest over 6–8 weeks in late spring/early summer, then stop cutting so the plants build up strength for next season's crop.

Where to grow: A sunny, sheltered spot with good drainage and fertile soil is ideal. A well-maintained bed should last for at least 20 years, but needs lots of space. In a small garden, grow one or two plants at the back of a border.

How to grow: Sow seed under heated glass in late winter and grow on until the plants are big enough to place in their permanent position the following spring. Plant the spidery crowns in trenches 8in (20cm) deep and 12in (30cm) wide, 3–3ft 4in (90–100cm) apart. Mound up the base of the trench about 3in (7cm) so the roots are spread over the mound and hang down towards the edges. Cover crowns with 2in (5cm) of sifted soil. Fill in the trench gradually as the plants grow. The bed should be level by early autumn.

Average yield: 20–25 spears per mature plant.

Maintenance: Water regularly and hand weed. Do not use a hoe as the roots are so near the surface. Stake the growing foliage. Top-dress the bed in spring with a thick layer of rotted manure. Cut the top growth down in the autumn when it turns yellow, and tidy up the bed.

Harvesting and storing: Cut the spears with a sharp knife 2–4in (5–10cm) below soil level when they are 4–6in (10–15cm) high. Cut frequently as the spears should not be allowed to grow too high. Asparagus is best eaten immediately but will keep for up to two weeks in a refrigerator (do not wash before storing). To freeze, blanch the spears for 2–4 minutes, depending on size.

Pests and diseases: Slugs, asparagus beetle, rust, violet root rot.

Other species and varieties:
Seed: 'Connover's Colossal' has mid-green, well-flavoured spears, and comes into full production from the fourth year.
'Jersey Knight F1' is an all-male hybrid. Its large, succulent green spears have purple-tinged tips.

Companion plants: Tomatoes, basil, parsley.

ABOVE **An asparagus bed in a sunny, sheltered spot**

NAME **AUBERGINE**
SOLANUM MELONGENA
FAMILY **SOLANACEAE**

Type: Short-lived perennial, grown as annual
USDA zone: 5 and above
Description: Aubergines are grown for their egg-shaped fruits. The skins are usually almost black, though there are white-skinned, cream and maroon striped varieties. Plants have attractive leaves and flowers.
Sowing and harvesting: Sow seed in spring for harvesting from late summer to mid-autumn.
Where to grow: Aubergines enjoy a sunny, sheltered position and a well-drained soil. They can also be planted in pots on a patio or in growing bags, 2–3 plants per bag. They need temperatures of 77–86°F (25–30°C). Plant outside when all danger of frost has passed.

How to grow: Sow seed under glass at a temperature of 60–70°F (15–21°C). Sow two seeds per pot and remove the weaker seedling. Harden off, and plant out under cloches in rows 24in (60cm) apart, allowing 24in (60cm) between each plant. Water in well. Cover the soil with cloches for 2–3 weeks before planting to warm it up. Leave cloches in place until the plants reach the top of the glass.
Average yield: 4–5lb (1.8–2.3kg) per plant.
Maintenance: Pinch out terminal growing points when the plants are 12in (30cm) high to encourage bushiness. When the fruits begin to swell, support the plants with canes and feed regularly with a liquid organic feed. Mist plants in hot weather and protect from wind, heavy rain, and low temperatures. When five fruits (depending on variety) have formed, remove the lateral shoots and remaining flowers.
Harvesting and storing: Cut each fruit when it has reached 5–6in (12–15cm) and is still shiny. Do not allow the fruits to become dull and over-ripe as they will taste bitter. They will stay fresh in a polythene bag in the refrigerator for up to two weeks.
Pests and diseases: Red spider, aphid, whitefly (greenhouse pest).
Other species and varieties:
'Black Beauty' (organic) is a medium-early variety that produces large numbers of oval- to globe-shaped, dark, glossy, violet fruit.
'Long Purple' (organic) has long, deep violet fruits with an excellent flavour.
'Violetta di Firenze' (organic) has round, ribbed, glossy violet fruit.
Companion plants: Beans, potatoes, marjoram.

ABOVE **The dark, shiny fruit of a 'Long Tom' F1 aubergine starting to form**

NAME **BEAN – BROAD**
VICIA FABA
FAMILY **LEGUMINOSAE**

Type: Hardy annual

USDA zone: 3 and above

Description: Broad beans are a hardy vegetable and can be round or kidney-shaped and white or green. Fragrant, white and black flowers are followed by leathery pods. About three or four square-sectioned stems grow from each plant.

Sowing and harvesting: Sow seed under cloches in late winter. Begin maincrop planting in early spring and then at monthly intervals until late spring for harvesting throughout summer into early autumn. In mild areas, the hardy 'Aquadulce Claudia' can be sown in late autumn/early winter to provide an early crop. Successive spring sowings will provide beans throughout the summer.

Where to grow: Broad beans prefer a rich, free draining, neutral or slightly alkaline soil in a reasonably sunny position. Avoid cold, wet soils. Broad beans take up a great deal of space and are not suitable for container growing. Dwarf varieties can be grown in gaps in beds and borders. Choose a dwarf variety for exposed sites.

How to grow: Sow the large seeds at 8in (20cm) intervals in double rows in drills 2in (5cm) deep and 8in (20cm) apart. Leave 2–3 ft (60–90 cm) between the double rows. Plant a few extra seeds in the space between the rows and transplant later to fill gaps if necessary.

Average yield: 20lb (9kg) per double row 10ft (3m) long.

Maintenance: Hoe regularly to remove weeds during the early stages. Watering should not be necessary before the flowers appear, but huge amounts of water will be needed if the weather is dry when the pods are swelling. Tall varieties will need support. Place a cane at the end of each row and tie string between them about 12in (30cm) above soil level. As the beans grow taller, add more string higher up the canes. As soon as the first beans begin to form, pinch off the top 3in (7cm) of stem to encourage pod development and discourage blackfly. After cropping, dig the plants into the soil to provide green manure, a valuable source of nitrogen.

Harvesting and storing: Broad beans are best picked young, before the skins become tough. If the scar on the bean is black, it has been left on the plant for too long. The tops of the plants can also be eaten. Broad beans freeze well.

Pests and diseases: Blackfly, black bean aphid, bean seed fly, chocolate spot.

Other species and varieties:

'Witkiem Manita' (organic) is a very early-maturing variety for spring sowing with large-podded, light green beans of excellent quality.

'Super Aquadulce' (organic) is a compact good-flavoured variety with long pods. It is the hardiest variety for autumn/early spring sowing.

'The Sutton' (non-organic) is a very hardy bush variety just 12in (30cm) tall, and is ideal for the small garden.

Companion plants: Brassicas, carrots, celery, corn, lettuce, potato.

ABOVE **Flowers starting to appear on the broad bean plants**

NAME **BEAN – FRENCH**
PHASEOLUS VULGARIS
FAMILY **LEGUMINOSAE**

Type: Half-hardy annual

USDA zone: 4 and above

Description: French beans are usually grown as compact bushes 12–18in (30–45cm) high, but climbing varieties can grow as tall as runner beans. Standard varieties are bushy, with 4–6in (10–15cm) green pods following white, pink or red flowers, though there are other variations of pod colour. They are highly decorative.

Sowing and harvesting: Sow inside in early spring and plant out in mid-spring for harvesting in summer. Sow outside throughout spring for harvesting from summer to mid autumn. Sow the maincrop in late spring, with successional sowings until early summer, for harvesting until mid-autumn.

Where to grow: French beans enjoy warm soil (pH6.5), in a reasonably sunny spot sheltered from high winds. Lime the soil in winter if necessary. They are decorative enough to be grown in the flower border.

How to grow: Sow under glass in early spring at a temperature of 65–70°F (18–21°C), two seeds to each 3in (7cm) pot. Thin out the weaker seedlings. In mid-spring, plant under cloches 8in (20cm) apart in rows 12in (30cm) apart. Sow the next crop under cloches in early spring, placing two seeds 8in (20cm) apart and 2in (5cm) deep in rows 12in (30cm) apart. Sow seed without cloches in mid spring. Sow bush varieties in staggered rows 6in (15cm) apart.

Average yield: Dwarf/bush varieties: 8lb (3.5kg) per 10ft (3m) row. Climbing varieties: 12lb (5.4kg) per 10ft (3m) row.

Maintenance: Hoe regularly in the early stages to keep the weeds down. Support plants with sticks, using plastic netting as well for climbing varieties. Water abundantly and regularly if the weather is dry during or after the flowering period to ensure maximum pod development. Mulch round the stems in early summer.

Harvesting and storing: Pick regularly when the pods are young and about 4in (10cm) long. Pick several times a week to stop them maturing, then cropping should continue for six or seven weeks. The beans freeze well. To obtain dried French beans (haricots), leave the pods on the stems until they are straw-coloured, then hang the plants indoors to dry. Shell when the pods are brittle and dry on a sheet of paper for several days. Store in an airtight jar.

Pests and diseases: Slugs, aphids, bean seed fly, halo blight, bean mosaic virus.

Other species and varieties:

Dwarf/bush: 'Slenderette' (organic) is a high-yielding maincrop variety with dark green, stringless pods that is very good for freezing.

'Opera' (organic) is a reliable cropper, ideal for organic growing, with round, dark green pods.

Climbing: 'Helda' (organic) is a medium-early variety that crops over a long period. It has flat pods that slice well and is resistant to bean mosaic virus.

'Eva' has early maturing, dark green, oval pods, and is resistant to bean, cucumber and yellow mosaic virus. It can also be grown in a greenhouse or polytunnel.

Companion plants: Cucumber, cauliflower, cabbage, carrot, marigold.

ABOVE **Dwarf French beans 'Firetongue'**

NAME **BEAN – RUNNER**
PHASEOLUS COCCINEUS
FAMILY **LEGUMINOSAE**

Type: Tender perennial, grown as an annual in temperate/cool climates

USDA zone: 4 and above

Description: Runner beans are climbers with long, flat pods and scarlet flowers. They can be seen in the summer growing up poles, wigwams and plastic netting.

Sowing and harvesting: Sow in late spring when all danger of frost is over, for harvesting from late summer to early/mid autumn.

Where to grow: Runner beans prefer a sheltered position and to succeed must have fertile, well-drained soil (pH6.5). Choose a spot where the dense shade they cast will not be a problem. The plants are decorative and tall enough to grow as screens. They can also be grown on patios in containers, and on cane 'wigwams' as a dense, highly-decorative cone.

How to grow: In early spring take out a trench one spit deep and 24in (60cm) wide. Dig in organic manure and refill with the original soil. Four or five weeks later, rake in a balanced organic fertilizer. Warm up the soil using cloches. Sow individual seeds 6in (15cm) apart in drills 2in (5cm) deep. Sow two drills 24in (60cm) apart for double-row growing. A variety such as 'Kelvedon Marvel' can be grown as a bush. For dwarf varieties, sow seed 6in (15cm) apart in rows 24in (60cm) apart. Pinch off the growing tip when the plant reaches 12in (30cm). Remove any climbing shoots regularly. Dwarf bushes will start cropping two weeks earlier.

Support: Apart from dwarf varieties, runner beans need support soon after they start growing. They can be trained up poles, strings or nets. Use 8ft (2.4m) canes crossed and tied at the top to form an inverted V-shape. Sow beans at 6in (15cm) intervals in the rows. Canes can be made into wigwams.

Average yield: 60lb (27kg) per 10ft (3m) double row.

Maintenance: Tie the young plants loosely to the supports to allow them to climb naturally and to protect them from slugs. As they grow, twist the plants anti-clockwise around the supports to encourage them to climb. Hoe regularly and water in dry weather once the pods have formed. Give a liquid feed occasionally during the cropping season. The plants can grow more than 10ft (3m) tall, but should be stopped when they reach the top of the support by pinching out the growing point. At the end of the growing season, dig the roots and stem bases into the ground.

RIGHT **Pods of the organic dwarf French bean 'Purple Queen'**

LEFT **Runner beans climbing up poles in the vegetable plot**

Harvesting and storing: Pick regularly once the pods are about 6–8in (15–20cm) long, but before the beans inside have started to swell. If pods are allowed to ripen the plants will stop production, so harvest virtually every other day. If you do this, you should be able to continue harvesting for at least two months. You may end up with a glut, but runner beans freeze well.

Pests and diseases: Blackfly, bean seed fly, red spider mite, halo blight in wet or humid weather.

Other species and varieties:

'Scarlet Emperor' (organic) is a traditional early variety chosen by many gardeners for its flavour.

'Enorma Elite' (organic) has slim, stringless pods produced over a long period. The beans are of a superior quality.

'White Emergo' (organic) has white flowers and smooth pods when young. It is high-yielding with a very pleasant flavour.

'Hestia' (organic) is a dwarf variety with lovely red and white flowers and slim, stringless pods, that can be grown in containers.

Companion plants: Cauliflower, cabbage, carrot, cucumber, marigold, rosemary, radish.

ABOVE **The scarlet flowers of the runner bean 'Kelvedon Marvel'**

NAME **BEETROOT (BEET)**
BETA VULGARIS SUBSP. VULGARIS
FAMILY **CHENOPODIACEAE**

Type: Half-hardy perennial, grown as annual

USDA zone: Almost all. Where summers are hot, 8 and above

Description: Beetroot is a relation of Swiss chard and has the same bright red coloration. Its edible roots can be round, long or tapering.

Sowing and harvesting: Seed is slow to germinate. Soak in warm water before sowing to speed up the process. Sow outdoors in mid-spring and again in late spring for a regular supply of roots. For a very early crop, sow a bolt-resistant variety under glass in early spring and harvest in early summer. For winter storage, sow in early summer and harvest in autumn.

ABOVE **Beetroot growing in the vegetable plot**

Where to grow: Beetroot likes well-prepared, preferably light, well-drained soil in an open, sunny position. Use a plot into which organic matter has been dug the previous autumn. It can also be grown in raised beds. It grows well in containers and its leaves look decorative in the flower border. It is good for intercropping. Young plants are sensitive to cold.

How to grow: Sow directly into shallow drills ½–¾in (12–18mm) deep and 12in (30cm) apart. Or station-sow two seeds at 4in (10cm) intervals, and thin out when large enough to handle leaving a single seedling at each station.

Average yield: 10lb (4.5kg) per 10ft (3m) row (globe); 18lb (8.2kg) per 10ft (3m) row (long).

Maintenance: Keep plants weed free, but take care when using a hoe. Water every two weeks in dry weather but water sparingly as too much increases leaf growth rather than root size.

Harvesting and storing: Pull out the roots of globe varieties when they are the size of tennis balls. Remove long varieties using a fork carefully so the prongs do not touch the roots. Twist off the foliage, leaving a 2in (5cm) crown of stalks. Do not cut leaves with a knife or the roots will 'bleed'. Roots can be left in the ground

until required. In cold areas, or if grown for storage, lift in autumn and store in boxes in layers of dry peat in a dry, frost-free shed or garage. Roots will stay fresh for up to two weeks in a polythene bag in the refrigerator.

Pests and diseases: Mangold fly (leaf miner), heart rot, leaf spot, black leg, speckled yellows, fanging, bolting.

Other species and varieties:

'Early Wonder' (organic) has good, large, globe-shaped sized roots, and can be used for both early and maincrop sowing.

'Boltardy' resists bolting and is a good red colour, with medium sized, globe-shaped roots.

'Cylindra' (organic) has long roots, dark red flesh and smooth, dark skin. It can be harvested over a long period and stores well.

'Forono' is ideal for slicing and pickling, gives good yields and has a good flavour.

Companion plants: Kohl rabi, onions, chives, dwarf beans.

NAME BROCCOLI – CALABRESE
BRASSICA OLERACEA ITALICA GROUP
FAMILY CRUCIFERAE

Type: Hardy annual/biennial
USDA zone: 3 and above
Description: Calabrese has a compact green terminal head and side shoots. It is also known as Italian sprouting broccoli and sometimes American broccoli. It should not be grown where the mean temperature is above 59°F (15°C).
Sowing and harvesting: Sow in succession from spring to early summer for harvesting during summer and autumn. Calabrese will be ready for harvesting 10–12 weeks after sowing. 'Romanesco' will be ready to harvest from late autumn to early winter or even later if it is protected by cloches.
Where to grow: Calabrese enjoys an open site and fertile soil that has been manured during the previous autumn, or for a previous crop.

How to grow: Either sow broadcast or station sow (three seeds per station) in shallow ½in (12mm) drills. For larger plants, thin the seedlings to 12in (30cm) apart in rows 12in (30cm) apart. Sow where the plants are to mature as they do not transplant well. After germination, remove the weakest seedlings, leaving only the strongest at each station.
Average yield: 1lb 8oz (675g) per plant.
Maintenance: Weed and water the plants well. Cut the terminal heads to encourage side shoots to develop, then apply an organic liquid feed.
Harvesting and storing: Calabrese first produces a single head, which should be cut when it is tightly closed. Later, some varieties produce side shoots with smaller heads. 'Romanesco' produces only one head per plant, so after harvesting this, dig up the plant and add it to the compost heap. Eat fresh, as it will not keep for more than a few days in the refrigerator. It can be frozen.
Pests and diseases: Slugs, snails, cabbage root fly, caterpillars, aphids, club root, whiptail.
Other species and varieties:
'Green Comet' is an F1 variety with a large central head up to 7in (17cm) across. It is an early cropper and there is little spear production after cutting the main head.
'Veronica F1' stands well, has attractive fresh green florets and nice curds, and is suitable for late summer and autumn.
'Waltham' (organic) is a fast-growing, traditional green calabrese.
'Romanesco' is a Roman variety with large, yellow-green pyramid-shaped heads.
Companion plants: Celery, rosemary, lettuce, chamomile, onions, potatoes, tomatoes.

ABOVE **Calabrese spears**

NAME **BROCCOLI – SPROUTING**
BRASSICA OLERACEA CYMOSA GROUP
FAMILY **CRUCIFERAE**

Type: Hardy or half-hardy biennial

USDA zone: 3

Description: Sprouting broccoli has loose green sprouting heads, each of which is a mass of flower buds, at the end of a soft stalk. The head and st`lk are eaten, along with some of the leaves. Most varieties of sprouting broccoli produce a mass of smaller heads on lots of side shoots rather than one large head. Purple sprouting broccoli is the most popular variety, but there is also a white form. Sprouting broccoli can grow to 3ft (90cm) with a spread of up to 2ft (60cm).

Sowing and harvesting: Sow early purple sprouting broccoli in spring and plant out in summer for harvesting in early spring the following year. Sow purple sprouting broccoli in spring and plant out in summer for harvesting in mid-spring the following year.

Where to grow: Sprouting broccoli enjoys a rich, firm soil and a sunny site. Dig the soil in autumn and work in plenty of organic matter.

How to grow: Sow seed thinly in shallow drills 6in (15cm) apart and $\frac{1}{2}$in (12mm) deep. Thin the seedlings to about 3in (7cm) apart. When they are 3in (7cm) high transplant them to their permanent position. Plant them firmly about 1in (2.5cm) deeper than they were in the drills. Allow 18in (45cm) between each plant.

Average yield: 1lb 8oz (675g)/10ft (3m) row.

Maintenance: Water regularly, particularly in dry weather. Cover the soil with organic matter or black polythene to conserve moisture. Hoe regularly and protect young plants from birds. Prevent from flowering by pinching out the buds, because once in flower the spears become tasteless and woody. If the temperature goes too high the plants will bolt.

Harvesting and storing: Broccoli sends up a central stalk that bears a cluster of flower buds (spears). Harvest this unopened central part with 6–8in (15–20cm) of stem. After the main stem is cut, the side branches lengthen and the plant produces smaller clusters for harvesting throughout the growing season. Broccoli will stay fresh in a refrigerator for up to three days. It freezes well.

Pests and diseases: Slugs, snails, pigeons, cabbage butterfly, cabbage moth, cabbage root fly, club root.

Other species and varieties:

'Purple Sprouting Early' (organic) produces a steady supply of shoots in early spring and turns bright green when cooked.

'Purple Sprouting Late' is similar to the early variety but harvesting begins in mid-spring and it crops over a longer period than hybrids.

Companion plants: Dill, celery, chamomile, sage, rosemary.

ABOVE **Sprouting broccoli**

NAME **BRUSSELS SPROUT**
BRASSICA OLERACEA GEMMIFERA GROUP
FAMILY **CRUCIFERAE**

Type: Hardy biennial, grown as annual

USDA zone: 4–7

Description: Brussels sprouts are large, leafy plants. Crisp, tasty buds or 'buttons' like miniature cabbages develop on the stem from the bottom upwards. They vary from about 14in (35cm) to 30in (75cm) high. Both dwarf and tall forms have a spread of up to 20in (50cm).

Sowing and harvesting: Early varieties grow faster, but are shorter and have lower yields. Plant in late winter/early spring and harvest in late summer/early autumn. Late varieties are hardier, taller and higher-yielding. Plant in spring and harvest from late autumn through to spring.

Where to grow: Sprouts enjoy an open, sheltered position in full sun and deeply-dug, fertile soil. Avoid exposed, windy situations and poorly drained or light soil. The roots need depth to support the long season of growth.

How to grow: Sow seed thinly in ¾–1in (18mm–2.5cm) drills, 2–3ft (60–90cm) apart. Thin to 15–24in (37–60cm) apart. Or sow in seed trays and transplant at the same distances directly into the ground. Spacing and growing conditions can affect the size of the buttons. Catch crop between rows with salad crops such as radishes, mustard and cress and lettuces.

Average yield: 2lbs (900g) per plant.

Maintenance: Keep the soil moist and weed regularly. Mulch to conserve moisture with straw or mushroom compost. Earth up the stems of the tall varieties as they grow to ensure stability. Remove and dispose of yellowing leaves. Cover with netting to protect from birds.

Harvesting and storing: Harvest the buttons as soon as they are large enough. Snap off from the bottom of the stalk upwards. They can be left on the stems until needed. After harvesting, dig up the plant, break up the stem and add to the compost heap. Sprouts freeze well.

Pests and diseases: Flea beetle, cabbage root fly, cabbage aphids, cabbage caterpillars, powdery mildew.

Other species and varieties:

Early: 'Darkmar 21' (organic) produces dark green, well-flavoured sprouts and crops heavily. 'Early Half Tall' is an open-pollinated type that gives a heavy crop.

Late:'Igor F1' (organic) grows to 32in (80cm) tall, produces mid-green, tight, round buttons, and has good frost tolerance.

'Wellington F1' is a hardy, mildew-resistant variety with tight, dark green buttons. Harvest from early winter to early spring.

Companion plants: Hyssop, sage, thyme, potatoes.

ABOVE **Large, leafy Brussels sprouts**

NAME **CABBAGE**
BRASSICA OLERACEA CAPITATA GROUP
FAMILY **CRUCIFERAE**

Type: Hardy biennial, usually grown as annual
USDA zone: 3 and above
Description: Cabbage heads can be round or pointed with dark or light green, blue-green, white or red leaves that are smooth or crinkled. They grow to 8–10in (20–25cm) with a spread of up to 28in (70cm). An average head is about 6in (15cm) in diameter.
Sowing and harvesting:
Spring cabbage: sow in late summer for harvesting in spring.
Summer cabbage: sow in the greenhouse in early spring. Harden off in a cold frame.
Red: sow in spring for harvesting in autumn.
Savoy: sow in spring for harvesting in late autumn/early winter.
Winter: sow in spring for harvesting in winter.

Where to grow: Cabbages enjoy a firm, fertile, well-drained soil in a reasonably sunny spot.
How to grow: Sow seed thinly in drills ½–1in (18mm–2.5cm) deep, 6in (15cm) apart. Transplant large-headed varieties in rows 18in (45cm) apart at 18in (45cm) intervals. Transplant smaller-headed varieties in rows 14in (35cm) apart at 14in (35cm) intervals. Plant spring cabbage in rows 12in (30cm) apart, leaving just 4in (10cm) between plants; the thinnings will provide spring greens.
Average yield: 12oz–3lbs (350g–6.6kg) per plant.
Maintenance: Keep the soil moist and weed carefully. In autumn, protect from birds with plastic netting, and earth up the stems of spring cabbage. In winter, firm down any plants loosened by wind or frost.

ABOVE **Well-hearted summer cabbages**

95

Harvesting and storing: Cut cabbages as soon as the hearts begin to firm and before they split or crack, using a sharp knife to cut cleanly through the stem just below the bottom leaves. Store on a chicken wire rack in an airy, frost-free place; they should keep for several weeks. Trim the remaining stalks and make a cross-shaped cut in the top; leave to overwinter and produce shoots in spring as a source of spring greens, or chop up and add to the compost heap.

Pests and diseases: Cabbage white caterpillars, maggots of the cabbage root fly, flea beetles, white fly, white aphid, club root.

Other species and varieties:

'Spring Hero F1' is a spring cabbage with a good-sized ball head.

'Myatt's Offenham' (organic) is dark green, quick-hearting and not prone to bolting.

'Derby Day' (organic) is one of the best early summer ball-head cabbages.

'Premiere' (organic) has medium-sized, crisp, round heads and very good texture and flavour.

'January King' has red-tinged hearts and good frost resistance.

'Celtic F1' is an outstanding grower and does not split readily.

'Vertus' (organic) is a Savoy variety that withstands severe frosts, and is ideal when little else is available.

'Marner Fruerot' (organic) is a very early red variety with medium-sized heads.

'Marner Lagerrot' (organic) has a uniform, red ball-head and stores well.

Companion plants: Beetroot, potatoes, beans, onions, sage, hyssop, chamomile, mint, rosemary, coriander.

NAME **CARDOON**
CYNARA CARDUNCULUS
FAMILY **COMPOSITAE**

Type: Frost-tender perennial

USDA zone: 5 and above

Description: The flower heads of cardoons look like small globe artichokes, to which they are related, but they are grown for their edible, fleshy stem bases. They can reach 6ft (1.8m).

Sowing and harvesting: Sow seed in mid-spring for blanching in early autumn and harvesting five weeks later.

Where to grow: Cardoons enjoy a rich, well-drained soil (pH6). Plant in a trench to ensure ample moisture during the summer months. They need a long, mild growing season and are suitable for the back of the flower border.

How to grow: Dig trenches 12in (30cm) deep and 30in (75cm) apart, incorporating plenty of well-rotted manure as you dig. Sow about 1/4in (6mm) deep and 18in (45cm) apart in groups of three or four. Thin, leaving the strongest seedling at each station. In areas where winters are cold and the growing season is short, start seed indoors. Sow 1/4in (6mm) deep in small pots. Harden off plants when they are 3in (7cm) tall. Plant out when all danger of frost has passed.

Average yield: 1–2lb (450–900g) per plant.

Maintenance: Weed regularly and keep the soil moist. Half-strength organic liquid fertilizer can be applied at weekly intervals. To blanch, tie back the stalks with string and wrap the stems of each plant first with newspaper, then black polythene. Tie loosely. Hoe up the soil round the base of each plant. Do not cover the leaf tips.

Harvesting and storing: Dig up the roots five weeks after blanching and remove the outer leaves. Dig as required until the first frosts arrive. The tender young inner stems may be frozen.

Pests and diseases: Relatively few, but aphids can be a nuisance. Winter wet combined with the cold can make the plants rot.

Other species and varieties:
'Gigante di Romagna' is a decorative, architectural variety, ideal for the back of the flower border.

'Plein Blanc Enorme' is a French variety that produces huge, succulent stem bases

Companion plants: Nasturtiums, petunias, marigolds.

NAME **CARROT**
DAUCUS CAROTA
FAMILY **UMBELLIFERAE**

Type: Hardy biennial, grown as an annual

USDA zone: 3

Description: Carrots are grown for their orange roots, which vary in length according to variety. They have bright green, feathery foliage.

Sowing and harvesting: For a very early crop, sow a short-rooted variety under glass in early spring for harvesting in early summer. For an early crop, sow a summer short-rooted variety in a sheltered position from mid-spring for harvesting in mid-summer. For main crop carrots, sow intermediate- or long-rooted varieties between mid-spring and early summer for harvesting in early to mid-autumn. For a tender crop, sow a short-rooted variety in late summer and cover with cloches from mid-autumn.

Where to grow: Carrots enjoy a well drained, medium-texture, stone-free soil that has not been manured for at least a year before sowing. They prefer an open, sunny position. If your soil is heavy or stony, grow short-rooted varieties.

How to grow: Dig the soil in autumn. Prepare the seed bed in spring, working soil to a fine tilth. Sow seed thinly at a depth of $\frac{1}{2}$in (12mm) in rows 6in (15cm) apart. Thin out the seedlings to 2–3 in (5–7cm) apart.

Average yield:
Early crop: 8lb (3.5kg) per 10ft (3m) row.
Main crop: 10lb (4.5kg) per 10ft (3m) row.

Maintenance: Water during dry weather, and hand weed between plants. Burn or bury thinnings as the bruised foliage will attract carrot fly. Severe frosts will destroy the foliage and any exposed roots.

ABOVE **Leafy, green carrots growing in the vegetable plot**

ABOVE **A bunch of fresh carrots**

Harvesting and storing: Pull up small carrots from early summer. Use a fork to lift the main crop roots in mid-autumn. Cut the foliage to within about 1/2in (12mm) of the crown and store the crop in a wooden box between layers of sand in a dry, airy place. Carrots freeze well.

Pests and diseases: Carrot fly, violet root rot, sclerotinia rot, black rot, motley dwarf virus, fanging.

Other species and varieties:

'Nantes 2' (organic) is a fast-maturing early variety with blunt-ended, cylindrical roots and a lovely sweet flavour.

'Amsterdam Forcing' (organic) has small cylindrical roots, is the earliest variety for spring sowing, and is excellent for freezing.

'Chantenay' (organic) is an early maincrop variety with short, wedge-shaped roots. It is fast-growing and high yielding.

'Resistafly F1'(organic) has long, well-coloured, sweet juicy roots and good carrot fly tolerance. It is suitable for producing baby carrots.

'Cubic' (organic) is a deep red late maincrop variety with short, heavily-tapered roots and strong tops. It is excellent for long-term storage.

'Berlicum' (organic) is a high-quality red-orange late maincrop ideal for slicing.

Companion plants: Peas, cabbage, leaf lettuce, chives, coriander, rosemary, sage, leeks.

NAME **CAULIFLOWER**
BRASSICA OLERACEA BOTRYTIS GROUP
FAMILY **CRUCIFERAE**

Type: Hardy annual/hardy biennial

USDA zone: 3 and above

Description: Cauliflowers are considered the most difficult members of the brassica family to grow. They usually have creamy or white heads or curds about 8in (20cm) across, surrounded by green leaves but some varieties have green or purple heads. They grow to 18–24 in (45–60 cm) with a spread of up to 3ft (90cm).

Where to grow: Cauliflowers need a firm, settled, fertile non-acid soil. All but winter and early spring varieties need an open, sunny site.

How to grow: Prepare soil thoroughly, incorporating plenty of organic matter. Sow very thinly, cover with sifted soil, and firm down after planting. Transplant seedlings to about 2ft (60cm) apart. Plant firmly and water well to speed up establishment.

Average yield: 1–2lbs (450–900g) per plant.

Maintenance: Water well, particularly in the early stages. Protect summer varieties from sun by bending a few leaves over developing curds;

protect winter ones from the snow by breaking a few leaves over the curds. Hoe regularly to keep down weeds. Draw a little soil around the roots of each cauliflower, and press it down with your heel to prevent the wind rocking the plant. Water regularly throughout the growing season. Apply a liquid seaweed fertilizer if necessary.

Harvesting and storing: Harvest in the early morning if possible. Cut horizontally at the base of the stem using a sharp knife before the curd opens. Store upside-down, with the roots intact, in a dark place. Cauliflowers freeze well.

Pests and diseases: Cabbage root fly, flea beetle, cabbage caterpillars, birds, cabbage aphis, gall weevil, club root, downy mildew, wirestem, ringspot, whiptail.

Other species and varieties:

'Vroege Mechelse 2' (organic) is a very hardy summer variety with well-shaped, medium-sized, firm white heads that will tolerate cold and wet.

'Flora Blanca' (organic) is an older variety with good-quality white heads, slow to grow but a reliable autumn cropper.

'Celebrity' (organic) is a winter variety with pure white heads.

'Purple Cape' (organic) has rich purple heads with a distinctive flavour.

Sowing and harvesting:

Summer varieties: sow under glass in winter and transplant seedlings in spring for a summer crop. Sow outdoors in early spring, transplant in early summer for a late summer/ early autumn crop.

Autumn varieties: sow outdoors in spring and transplant in early summer for harvesting in autumn/early winter.

Winter varieties: sow outdoors in mid- to late spring. Transplant in mid-summer for harvesting in winter/early spring.

Companion plants: Celery, celeriac, beans, oregano, tansy, thyme.

LEFT Cauliflower 'All the Year Round' with a button head

NAME CELERIAC (CELERY ROOT)
APIUM GRAVEOLENS VAR. RAPACEUM
FAMILY UMBELLIFERAE

Type: Hardy biennial, grown as an annual
USDA zone: 5 and above
Description: Celeriac is a close relation of celery. It has a celery-flavoured 'bulb' at the base of the stem and needs a long growing season.
Sowing and harvesting: Sow under glass from late winter to early spring. Germination may be erratic. Harden off the plants in late spring. Harvest from autumn onwards.
Where to grow: Celeriac enjoys a rich, fertile, moisture-retentive soil and a sunny position.
How to grow: To produce a good root system, sow seed in trays and place in a propagator kept at a steady temperature of 61°F (16°C). Prick out the seedlings when they are large enough to handle, into 3in (7cm) pots. Plant one seedling per pot. Harden them off, then plant out 12in (30cm) apart, in rows 18in (45cm) apart, with the stem base at ground level.
Average yield: 7lbs (3.2kg) per 10ft (3m) row.
Maintenance: Hoe regularly and keep the ground moist as the plants develop. Mulch in early summer and feed occasionally. Remove side shoots, and remove the lower leaves from midsummer on to expose the crowns. If the crop is left in the ground, protect it from severe weather with straw.
Harvesting and storing: Dig up the plants, twist off the tops, and cut off the bulbs. Leave the bulbs in the ground until required, or lift and store them in boxes of damp peat in a cool shed or garage. Blanch cubes of celeriac and freeze on open trays.

Pests and diseases: Carrot fly, celery fly, slugs can be a problem with young plants.
Other species and varieties: 'Prinz' (organic) has large, round roots and crisp, white flesh. 'Marble Ball' has a strong flavour and stores well over winter. 'Jose' (early) has bulbs of uniform shape.
Companion plants: Leeks, beans, cabbage, tomatoes, dill.

NAME CELERY
APIUM GRAVEOLENS VAR. DULCE
FAMILY UMBELLIFERAE

Type: Biennial
USDA zone: 5 and above
Description: Celery has crisp leaf stalks that can be cooked or eaten raw. There are white, pink and red varieties. Red is the hardiest and white the best quality.
Sowing and harvesting: Sow seed under heated glass in early to mid-spring. Self-blanching varieties will be ready for harvesting between late summer and mid-autumn. Trench varieties can be harvested from late autumn.
Where to grow: Celery prefers a rich, well-drained soil (pH6.5–7) and an open site. Traditionally, it is grown in trenches to blanch the stems. Self-blanching varieties are less hardy.
How to grow: Sow seed under glass and harden off before planting outside. Seedlings are ready to transplant when they have five or six leaves. For trench varieties, dig a trench 12in (30cm) deep and 15in (37cm) wide. Fork the bottom and place a layer of manure over it, then fill to within 3in (7cm) of the top with soil. Allow to settle until planting time. Rake in some organic fertilizer before planting, and plant out 9in (23cm) apart. Fill the trench with water after

planting. Plant self-blanching varieties in a square block, spacing plants 9in (23cm) apart.

Average yield: 12lbs (5.5kg) per 10ft (3m) row.

Maintenance: Water all varieties abundantly in dry weather and give a liquid feed during the summer months. When trench varieties are around 12in (30cm) high, remove any side shoots and blanch by surrounding the stalks with corrugated cardboard tied loosely, then filling the trench with soil. In late summer, mound up the stems with moist soil and in early autumn finish earthing up so that there is a steep-sided mound with just the foliage tops showing. Cover the tops with straw during frosts. For self-blanching varieties, tuck straw between the plants on the outside line of the bed.

Harvesting and storing: Lift self-blanching varieties using a trowel, lifting the outer plants first. Complete harvesting before the first frosts. Harvest trench varieties according to type.

Pests and diseases: Celery fly (leaf miner), slugs and snails, celery heart rot, celery leaf spot (blight), splitting, bolting.

Other species and varieties:

'Solid Pink' (organic) is a hardy trench variety that stays red when cooked.

'Golden Self Blanching' (organic) has yellow foliage, cream stalks and needs little or no earthing up.

'Green Utah' (organic) is mid-green with delicious, crisp, smooth long stalks and a good inner heart.

'Daybreak' (organic) produces long, smooth stalks. It is recommended for summer cropping.

Companion plants: Cabbage, leek, onion, spinach, tomatoes.

ABOVE **Celery seedlings hardened off before planting**

NAME: CHICORY
CICHORIUM INTYBUS
FAMILY: COMPOSITAE

Type: Hardy perennial
USDA zone: 3 and above
Description: Chicory has a distinctive bitter flavour and its young, blanched leaves are delicious in salads. There are red- and green-leaved varieties. It often has soft, hairy leaves and blue or pink flowers. It is a useful winter crop and nearly all varieties are hardy.
Sowing and harvesting: Plant forcing varieties in late spring/early summer for harvesting in late winter/early spring. Plant non-forcing varieties in mid-summer for harvesting in autumn/winter.
Where to grow: Chicory needs a sunny, open position, but it is not fussy about soil type. A rich, moisture-retentive soil is ideal. If left in the ground for a second year, it produces blue or pink flowers and is an attractive addition to the herbaceous border.
How to grow: Dig the soil in autumn/early winter, incorporating organic matter. Prepare the seed bed a few days before sowing. Sow the seed very thinly in drills ½in (12mm–2.5cm) deep in rows 12in (30cm) apart. Thin seedlings to 9in (23cm) apart.
Average yield: 6lbs (2.7kg) per 10ft (3m) row.
Maintenance: Hoe regularly to remove weeds. To encourage deep root growth, water only in dry weather, or when plants show signs of wilting. Protect from frost any plants that are not to be cut until the winter.
Harvesting and storing:
Forcing varieties: when the plants are about 6in (15cm) high dig them up, cut off the leaves just above the crown, and trim the bottom of the roots leaving about 12in (30cm) of the thickest parts. Plant 3in (7cm) apart in deep boxes of moist sandy soil or peat, so the crowns protrude above the surface. Some varieties will form tight chicons without a covering. Force in darkness, keeping the temperature above 50°F (10°C), or

they will be green and bitter. After about four weeks, the chicons should be about 7in (17cm) tall and fully formed. Break them off carefully just before you need them as they wilt very quickly. Breaking them off will encourage a smaller, second crop.

Non-forcing varieties: Cut heads in late autumn and use immediately, or store them in a cool shed. It will stay fresh in a black polythene bag in the refrigerator for up to four weeks.

Pests and diseases: Wireworms, cutworms, swift moth caterpillars. Slugs can ruin the leaves.

Other species and varieties:
'Witloof' is the traditional forcing variety and is sometimes called Belgian chicory.
'Normato' needs no soil layer when forcing.
'Sugar Loaf' is the traditional non-forcing variety.
'Crystal Head' is hardier than 'Sugar Loaf'.

Companion plants: Lavender, marigolds.

ABOVE **Chicory growing in the vegetable plot**

NAME **CHINESE CABBAGE**
BRASSICA RAPA VAR. PEKINENSIS
FAMILY: **CRUCIFERAE**

Type: Annual or biennial

USDA zone: 2 and above

Description: Most varieties of Chinese cabbage derive from Japanese cultivars and are grown as annuals. The heads are tightly packed with dense, pale, sweet-tasting creamy-yellow leaves, that are blanched through lack of light.

Sowing and harvesting: Sow seed in early/mid summer. Harvest from about seven weeks later and cut as required to late autumn.

Where to grow: Chinese cabbage enjoys a rich, fertile, moisture-retaining soil, and an open site with some shade. Grow alongside other brassicas, but in a special bed with plenty of manure or compost added, or in deep beds.

How to grow: Chinese cabbage will bolt if sown too early. Sow in shallow drills 12in (30cm) apart, thinning seedlings to 12in (30cm) apart, or in blocks, thinning to 9in (23cm) apart. It does not like being transplanted. Seed cannot be stored, so sow fortnightly for a succession.

Average yield: 12oz–3lbs (350g–1.35kg) per plant.

Maintenance: Hoe regularly to keep the crop weed free. Make sure the plants have plenty of water throughout their growth. If they start to bolt, treat them as a cut-and-come-again crop.

Harvesting and storing: Chinese cabbages mature quickly and can be cut at any stage. Harvest by cutting about 1in (2.5cm) above soil level. The stumps may resprout several times and form new leaves for harvesting.

Pests and diseases: Slugs, millipedes, cabbage caterpillars, flea beetles, club root.

Other species and varieties:

'Nikko' (organic) is a bolt-resistant, first-cropping cabbage with a delicious, dark green head. 'Wong Bok' has large, barrel-shaped heads weighing up to 5lbs 8oz (2.5kg), light green leaves and broad, white midribs.

'Tatsoi' (organic) is a loose-headed variety with spoon-shaped, dark green, glossy leaves. It crops well into winter.

Companion plants: Marigold, nasturtium, tomato, celery.

ABOVE **An organic Chinese cabbage with dark green, glossy leaves**

NAME **CORN /SWEET CORN/ MAIZE**
ZEA MAYS
FAMILY **GRAMINEAE**

Type: Half-hardy annual

USDA zone: 3 and above

Description: Corn or sweetcorn is a type of maize with broad, strap-like leaves and ears of soft, smooth yellow grains. The spikes of the male flowers (tassels) decorate the top of the plant, and the cobs, with their female flowers (silks) form where the leaves join the main stem. Plants grow to 5ft (1.5m) or more.

Sowing and harvesting: Sow seed in pots in the greenhouse in mid-spring. Plant out in late spring/early summer when all danger of frost has passed. Or sow seed outdoors under cloches in late spring. Harvest in autumn.

Where to grow: Corn enjoys full sun and shelter from the wind. It prefers warm, well-drained soil that does not dry out too quickly. It is pollinated by the wind, so grow it in compact blocks. Pollen from the male flowers at the top will fall and pollinate the female ones half-way down the

ABOVE Brown female silk, an indication that the cob is ready for harvesting

stems. Grow fast-growing salad crops or dwarf beans between the maturing plants. The plants are attractive and worth growing in the decorative kitchen garden.

How to grow: Sow two seeds together 2in (5cm) deep and at 12–18in (30–45cm) intervals each way, in a block rather than rows. Remove weaker seedlings after germination. Seed will not germinate in temperatures below 50°F (10°C) but the plants can be given an early start by pre-germinating or chitting. Once chitted, plant indoors 1in (2.5cm) deep, one to a pot, or outdoors in soil warmed by cloches.

Average yield: 1–2 cobs per plant.

Maintenance: In exposed areas, draw the soil about 6in (15cm) up the stems, to support growing established plants against the wind. Hand-weed rather than hoe to avoid severing surface anchorage roots. Keep plants moist when they are flowering and when the cobs are swelling.

Harvesting and storing: Harvest the cobs when the silks begin to turn brown. Test by peeling back the sheath and inserting your thumb into a kernel; if white sap comes out, they are ripe. Twist the cobs so that they snap off from the stem. For the best results, cook immediately. They can also be frozen.

Pests and diseases: Corn smut, frit fly, boron deficiency, mice, slugs and birds.

Other species and varieties:

'Sundance' is a slow-maturing mid-season variety suitable for cooler climates.

'Champ' is a reliable, early-maturing, sweet variety.

'Early Xtra Sweet' has grains that contain at least twice as much sugar as the normal varieties.

'Candle' has long cobs on medium-high plants.

Companion plants: Artichokes, cucumbers, melons, pumpkins, parsnips, potatoes, squash.

NAME **COURGETTE (ZUCCHINI)**
CUCURBITA PEPO
FAMILY **CUCURBITACEAE**

Type: Annual

USDA zone: 4 and above

Description: Courgettes or zucchini are smaller than marrows, with firmer flesh and a superior taste. The plants are bushy in habit.

Sowing and harvesting: Sow outdoors in late spring and harvest in mid summer. Or sow under glass in mid-spring, plant out in early summer and harvest from midsummer to late autumn.

Where to grow: Courgettes enjoy a well-drained soil, rich in organic matter. They need a sunny spot protected from strong winds.

How to grow: To sow under glass, place a single seed edgeways ½in (12mm) deep in a small compost-filled pot. Keep the temperature at 65°F (18°C). Harden off seedlings before planting outside. To prepare the bed, dig holes the width and depth of a spade and 24in (60cm) apart. Fill with rotted manure mixed with soil, leaving a low mound on top. Sprinkle with an organic fertilizer before planting. Outside, sow 2–3 seeds 1in (2.5cm) deep and 2–3in (5–7cm) apart in the centre of each mound of the bed. Thin to leave the strongest seedling.

Average yield: 16 courgettes per plant.

Maintenance: Keep the soil moist and water around, not over, the plants. Syringe in dry weather and mulch to conserve moisture before the fruit forms. If the weather is cold, fertilize the female flowers (with what looks like a tiny fruit at the base) by removing the male flowers, folding back the petals, and pushing them gently into the female flowers. Feed every two weeks with a liquid feed once the fruits begin to form.

Harvesting and storing: Cut the courgettes when they are 4in (10cm) long, preferably with a flower attached. Harvest regularly to encourage more fruits and handle carefully as they bruise easily. They freeze well.

Pests and diseases: Slugs, pollen beetles, cucumber mosaic virus.

Other species and varieties:

'Gold Bush' (organic) has a crisp texture and attractive, bright yellow fruits.

'Defender F1' (organic) is a very early variety with dark green fruits which resist cucumber mosaic virus.

'Nero di Milan' (organic) has dark green, cylindrical fruits and an erect, open habit. It is ideal for slicing and freezing.

Companion plants: Marjoram, corn, nasturtium.

ABOVE **A flower has developed on a courgette 'Ambassador' F1**

NAME **CUCUMBER, GREENHOUSE**
CUCUMIS SATIVUS
FAMILY **CUCURBITACEAE**

Type: Annual

USDA zone: 4 and above

Description: Cucumbers are warm-season crops grown for their green-skinned fruits, and eaten raw in salads. Greenhouse types are long-stemmed with long, cylindrical fruits.

Sowing and harvesting: Sow seed in late winter, and plant in a heated greenhouse in early spring or in an unheated greenhouse from late spring for cutting from early summer.

Where to grow: In growing bags in the greenhouse. Cucumbers need high humidity and a temperature of 70–80°F (20–26°C).

How to grow: Chit cucumber seeds between pieces of moist absorbent paper and leave in a warm place: 70°F (21°C). Sow each chitted seed ¾in (18mm) deep in small pots of compost. Plant two seedlings to a growing bag and water after planting. Keep the compost moist, and make sure that the greenhouse is well ventilated and the air moist.

Average yield: 25 cucumbers per plant.

Maintenance: Support the plants with canes. Pinch out the growing points when the main stems reach the greenhouse roof. Maintain a minimum temperature of 60°F (16°C) for standard and 70°F (21°C) for all-female varieties. Spray the floor to maintain high humidity. Pinch out the tip of each side shoot two leaves beyond a female flower (those with a tiny cucumber behind them). When the flowerless side shoots are 24in (60cm) long pinch out the tips. Remove male flowers (those with a long thin stalk) from standard varieties as fertilized fruit can be bitter. Feed with a liquid organic fertilizer every fortnight after the fruits begin to swell.

Harvesting and storing: Cut cucumbers with a sharp knife when they reach the required size. They will stay fresh in the refrigerator for up to a week. Do not freeze.

Pests and diseases: Eelworm, cucumber mosaic virus, red spider mite, anthracnose, sclerotina rot, black rot, whitefly, gummosis, powdery mildew.

Other species and varieties:

'Conqueror' is a standard variety that produces good sized, mid-green fruits and tolerates lower temperatures than other greenhouse varieties.

'Telegraph' produces straight, dark green fruits and is an old variety that is a good all-rounder.

'F1 Flamingo' (organic) is an all-female variety that produces high yields of long fruits. The plants are strong-growing, tolerate low light and are tolerant of mildew.

'F1 Cum Laude' (organic) is a high-yielding modern variety used by commercial growers. It is tolerant of powdery mildew and can also be grown in unheated greenhouses or polytunnels.

'F1 Media' (organic) is a modern variety used by commercial growers.

Companion plants: Marigolds, nasturtiums, tobacco plants, sunflowers, squash.

ABOVE **A flower has developed on a cucumber plant**

NAME **CUCUMBER, OUTDOOR**
CUCUMIS SATIVUS
FAMILY **CUCURBITACEAE**

Type: Frost-tender annual

USDA zone: 11

Description: Outdoor or ridge cucumbers are rough-skinned, spiny, and grow to around 4–6in (10–15cm) long. They have no frost tolerance and most are damaged if the temperature dips below 50°F (10°C).

Sowing and harvesting: Sow outdoors in late spring/early summer to begin harvesting in late summer. For an earlier crop sow seed under glass in late spring and plant out in early summer when all danger of frost has passed.

Where to grow: Soil must be rich in humus and well drained. Gherkin varieties can be grown successfully in 9in (23cm) pots and trained onto a cane and wire support. The apple variety can be grown up a tripod of canes.

How to grow: 10–14 days before planting, make holes 12in (30cm) wide and deep at 18in (45cm) intervals. Fill with organic manure and replace the soil to produce low mounds. Sow three seeds in each mound 1in (2.5cm) deep and 2–3in (5–7cm) apart. Cover with cloches. When the seedlings have produced their first true leaves, thin to leave the strongest one at each station.

Average yield: 10 cucumbers per plant.

Maintenance: Keep the soil moist and always water around the plants. Mist in dry weather. When the plants have developed 6–8 leaves pinch out the growing tip. Train the side shoots that develop up netting, or leave to trail over the ground. Pinch out shoots without flowers at the seventh leaf. In summer, before the fruit forms, place black polythene over the soil. This will conserve moisture, raise soil temperature, keep down weeds, and prevent the fruit from rotting. Feed regularly with a liquid feed once the fruits have started to swell. Never remove the male flowers; they are needed to fertilize the female flowers.

Harvesting and storing: Cut cucumbers with a sharp knife as required when they are 6–8in (15–20cm) long for ridge types, 4in (10cm) long for the gherkin, and the apple cucumbers when they are 50 per cent bigger than an egg. The harvesting period is relatively short; the first frosts will kill the plants. Cucumbers can be kept in the refrigerator for up to a week. They do not freeze well.

Pests and diseases: Eelworm, slugs and snails, cucumber mosaic virus, grey mould (*botrytis*), foot and root rots.

ABOVE **An outdoor cucumber growing in the ground**

107

Other species and varieties:
'Marketmore' (organic) is a standard ridge variety that produces dark green, cylindrical fruits, and is resistant to cucumber mosaic virus.
'Klaro F1' (organic) has compact plants with dark green fruit up to 10in (25cm) long.
'La Diva F1' has smooth, thin skin and is seedless and very tender when picked young.
'Crystal Lemon' has delicious pale, round fruit that should be picked when 3½–5in (9–12cm) in diameter. It is also known as 'Crystal Apple'.
'Vert Petit de Paris' (organic) is a small French gherkin type with a fine taste and prolific yield.
'Stimora Mix F1' (organic) is a productive variety that can be harvested for pickling when 1½–2in (4–5cm) long or grown to 4in (10cm) for slicing.
Companion plants: Marigolds, beans, peas, radish, celery, sunflower.

NAME ENDIVE
CICHORIUM ENDIVIA
FAMILY COMPOSITAE

Type: Hardy annual or hardy biennial
USDA zone: 4 and above
Description: Endive is a leafy vegetable with ruffled foliage that forms a flat or semi-upright rosette of leaves. It is used in salads, but must be blanched to be palatable.
Where to grow: Endive needs a rich, moisture-retentive soil (pH5–7) and semi-shade. In hot sun, it will run to seed and become bitter.
How to grow: Sow seed thinly ½in (12mm) deep in drills 12in (30cm) apart. Cover with fine soil and firm down the surface. Thin the seedlings to 9in (23cm) apart for the curly-leaved varieties and to 12in (30cm) for the broad-leaved varieties.
Average yield: 10–15 heads per 10ft (3m) row.

Maintenance: Hoe regularly. Water in dry weather and feed occasionally with a liquid fertilizer. About 12 weeks after sowing, begin to blanch selected plants: tie up the leaves (which must be dry) loosely with raffia and cover with a plastic flower pot, blocking any drainage holes. The heads will be ready in about 5 weeks in winter, 2–3 weeks in summer. Alternatively, place a plate over the centre of the plant for partial blanching. After about 10 days, the centre of the endive should be white.
Harvesting and storing: Cut the heads with a sharp knife when the leaves have turned creamy white. Mature curled varieties respond well to cut-and-come-again treatment. Use immediately if possible, or store in a black bag in the refrigerator for up to three days. Do not freeze.
Pests and diseases: Slugs can be a problem at blanching time, and occasionally aphids.
Other species and varieties:
'Moss Curled' has finely-divided, curled leaves.
'Pancalier' (organic) is a broad, bulky-headed variety with dark green, serrated outer leaves and creamy white hearts.
'Batavian Green' is probably the most popular broad-leaved endive.
'Cornet de Bordeaux' has dark green, crunchy leaves that form big, closed heads.

ABOVE **Endive 'Fine Maraichere' growing in a shady position**

Sowing and harvesting: Sow in late spring for harvesting in summer, and in summer for an autumn/winter crop. For successive cropping, sow every 3–4 weeks from early spring to late autumn.

Companion plants: Chervil, poached egg plants, coriander.

NAME **FLORENCE FENNEL**
FOENICULUM VULGARE VAR. DULCE
FAMILY **UMBELLIFERAE**

Type: Half-hardy annual
USDA zone: 4 and above
Description: Florence fennel is grown for its aniseed-flavoured, bulb-like swollen leaf bases. Its attractive fern-like foliage can be used for flavouring.

Sowing and harvesting: Sow seed in mid- to late spring for a summer crop, and in early to mid-summer for an autumn crop. It will bolt if sown too early.

Where to grow: Florence fennel likes full sun and needs a warm summer for bulb development. It prefers very fertile, moisture-retentive but well-drained soil (pH6–7) into which plenty of organic matter has been worked. It has low nitrogen requirements.

How to grow: Sow seed in the greenhouse in mid-spring for the earliest crops. Choose a bolt-resistant variety and plant in modules. Harden the plants off carefully in late spring. For later crops, sow in open ground, thinly in drills 1/2in (12mm) deep. Thin seedlings to 9in (23cm) apart when large enough to handle and plant in rows 18in (45cm) apart. Florence fennel does not transplant well and may 'bolt' if checked; if possible sow where it is to be grown.

Average yield: 12–13 bulbs per 10ft (3m) row.

Maintenance: Keep well watered and weeded. When the stem base begins to swell, pile up the soil around the stem to blanch it. Continue the process throughout the summer.

Harvesting and storing: Harvest the bulbs when they are plump, fleshy and about the size of a tennis ball. Cut just above soil level and trim off the leaves. The stump can be left in the ground to produce a crop of smaller shoots.

Pests and diseases: Slugs.

Other species and varieties:
'Finale' (organic) produces firm, heavy, uniform bulbs and has excellent bolt resistance.
'Romanesco' (organic) is a 'sweet Florence' type with big white bulbs up to 2lbs 4oz (1kg).

Companion plants: Most plants dislike fennel so plant alone.

ABOVE **Organic Florence fennel 'Perfection' growing in full sun**

NAME **KALE**
BRASSICA OLERACEA ACEPHALA GROUP
FAMILY **CRUCIFERAE**

Type: Hardy annual or hardy biennial

USDA zone: all zones

Description: Most types of kale have dark green, crinkly leaves, apart from rape kale which has plain, uncrinkled leaves. Heights range from 12–16in (30–40cm) for dwarf kale to 3ft (90cm) or even more, depending on the variety. They are the hardiest of the brassicas, and some will tolerate temperatures as low as 5°F (–15°C).

Sowing and harvesting:

Sow curly-leaved kale in spring for harvesting in late autumn/winter.

Sow leaf and spear or plain-leaved kale in late spring for harvesting in late autumn/winter.

Sow rape kale in early summer for harvesting in late autumn/winter.

Where to grow: Kale will grow in most types of soil as long as there is satisfactory drainage. It likes an open situation.

How to grow: Sow seed very thinly, 1/2in (12mm) deep and in drills 6in (15cm) apart. Thin the seedlings to 3in (7cm) apart. Transplant to their permanent position when they are about 4–6in (10–15cm) high, planting them in rows 18in (45cm) apart. Thin the seedlings in stages until they are 18in (45cm) apart.

Average yield: 2lbs (900g) per plant.

Maintenance: Hoe and mulch the ground to keep free from weeds. Water regularly. Tread firmly round the plant stems to prevent them rocking in strong wind, and provide support on really exposed sites. Pick off any yellowing leaves and earth up around the stems in autumn.

Harvesting and storing: Snap off the leaves and use as required during autumn/winter, to encourage new growth. Pick shoots 4in (10cm) long in the spring, before the flowers open. Some varieties mature seven weeks after sowing, but can stand in the ground for a long time. Kale freezes well.

Pests and diseases: Kale is resistant to most of the problems that affect other brassicas, but whitefly, mealy aphid, and cabbage caterpillar can be a nuisance.

Other species and varieties:

'Dwarf Green Curled' (organic) is hardy, with tightly-curled, deep green leaves. It is suited to light soils, and good for small vegetable plots.

'Pentland Brig' (organic) is bred for texture and flavour. It produces young crown leaves in late autumn and leafy side shoots and spears that can be picked in spring.

'Cottagers' is a very hardy, old variety. It has plain leaves that turn bright purple in winter.

'Hungry Gap' is a robust, reliable late-cropping rape kale.

Companion plants: Thyme, sage.

RIGHT **Curly kale**

NAME **KOHL RABI**
BRASSICA OLERACEA GONGYLODES GROUP
FAMILY **CRUCIFERAE**

Type: Annual

USDA zone: 3 and above

Description: Kohl rabi has a turnip-like, swollen stem or 'globe' that forms just above ground. The outer skin is a greenish-white or purple and its white flesh can be eaten cooked or raw.

Sowing and harvesting: Sow white and green varieties between early spring and early summer for harvesting in autumn. Sow purple varieties in mid- to late summer for a late autumn or winter.

Where to grow: Kohl rabi prefers a sunny situation in fertile, well-drained soil (pH6–7), that is rich in humus.

How to grow: Sow seed thinly in drills $\frac{1}{2}$in (12mm) deep and 12in (30cm) apart, and cover with soil. Thin seedlings when the first true leaves appear, then at intervals until the plants are 6in (15cm) apart.

Average yield: 20 globes per 10ft (3m) row.

Maintenance: Hoe regularly. Feed occasionally with an organic fertilizer if growth is slow. Water very well during dry weather. Protect from birds.

Harvesting and storing: Harvest as needed from early summer when the globes are about the size of a tennis ball; they become woody if allowed to develop further. Pull as needed until early winter. Kohl rabi will stay fresh in the refrigerator in a plastic bag for up to two weeks. It can be frozen cut into strips.

Pests and diseases: Brassica pests and diseases are occasionally troublesome. Birds and aphids can be a nuisance.

Other species and varieties:

'Logo' (organic) is a fast-growing white variety with a flattened globe shape and excellent bolt-resistance.

'Olivia' is an early-maturing variety with large globes on firm stems and very white flesh. It is slow to bolt.

'Superschmelz' has pale green globes the size of a small football and crisp white flesh. It is resistant to bolting and splitting.

'Purple Vienna' has white flesh and purple skin. It is suitable for late sowing and winter harvest.

Companion plants: Marigolds, nasturtiums, beets, celery, onion, tomatoes, all strong herbs.

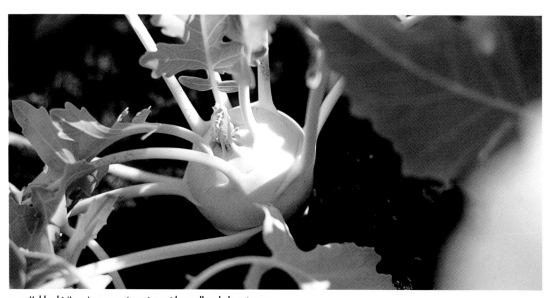

ABOVE **Kohl rabi 'Logo' an organic variety with excellent bolt resistance**

NAME **LAMB'S LETTUCE/CORN SALAD/MACHE**
VALERIANELLA LOCUSTA
FAMILY **VALERIANACEAE**

Type: Hardy annual

USDA zone: 2 and above

Description: Lamb's lettuce can be cropped all year round. There is a floppy, large-leaved variety and a smaller upright variety, with darker leaves. It can be used as a substitute for lettuce.

Sowing and harvesting: Sow in summer and autumn for harvesting from summer to spring.

Where to grow: Corn salad will grow in all types of soil if it is free-draining. For a summer salad crop, deep, fertile soil will ensure rapid growth. It may be grown as a 'cut and come again' seedling crop, in containers, used for inter-cropping and under-cropping vegetables such as winter brassicas, sown in blocks, and is useful where space is limited. It can be sown late in the season when the ground is cleared of summer crops.

How to grow: Take out drills ½in (12mm) deep and 4in (10cm) apart. Sow seed thinly and cover with sifted soil. When seedlings are 2in (5cm) tall, thin out to 4in (10cm) apart. Summer crops will benefit from a dressing of a balanced, general organic fertilizer before sowing.

Average yield: From 25–30 heads per 10ft (3m) row.

Maintenance: Keep well weeded, and water in dry weather. Use cloches to protect the crop from frost from mid-autumn onwards.

Harvesting and storing: Gather individual leaves or cut the whole plant as needed. It will crop most heavily in spring as the plants are preparing to flower. In winter, never remove more than two or three leaves at a time from each plant.

Pests and diseases: Generally trouble-free.

Other species and varieties:

'Vert de Cambrai' is a traditional French variety with a good flavour that produces hardier plants for winter growing.

'D'Olanda' (organic) is a very hardy green salad crop, very high in vitamins and minerals and with a good flavour.

'Vit' (organic) has long, glossy green leaves and a mild, minty flavour, and is ideal for over-wintering.

Companion plants: Brassicas, tomatoes, lettuce, onions.

ABOVE **Lamb's lettuce**

NAME **LEEK**
ALLIUM PORRUM
FAMILY **ALLIACEAE**

Type: Hardy biennial (grown as an annual)

USDA zone: 3 and above

Description: Leeks have long, blue-green leaves above edible thick, white stems or shanks of rolled leaves, and are one of the most reliable winter crops. The season lasts for more than six months.

Sowing and harvesting: Sow seed outdoors in late spring. Transplant seedlings in early summer for harvesting in autumn right through to spring.

ABOVE **Baby leeks 'King Richard' growing in a container**

Where to grow: Leeks will grow in any reasonable soil, provided that it is well drained. The crop prefers a sunny spot. Grow leeks in the border where their strap-shaped, blue-green leaves will add winter interest.

How to grow: Sow seed very thinly in drills ½in (12mm) deep and 6in (15cm) apart. Cover with soil. Thin seedlings to 1½in (37mm) apart. Transplant when they are around 8in (20cm) high and the thickness of a pencil. In dry weather, water the bed the day before transplanting. Trim off the root ends and leaf tips and plant 6in (15cm) apart in rows 12in (30cm) apart. Make a 6in (15cm) hole with a dibber, insert the leek and fill the hole with water, but not with soil.

Average yield: 10lbs (4.5kg) per 10ft (3m) row.

Maintenance: Water in dry weather and hoe to keep down weeds, but avoid getting soil in the holes. Blanch stems by drawing dry soil around the stems of well-developed plants at intervals until mid-autumn, increasing the height a little at a time. Try not to let soil to fall between the leaves as this will result in grittiness. Feed plants with an organic fertilizer to thicken the stems, but avoid late feeding if plants are to overwinter in the garden.

Harvesting and storing: Begin harvesting in autumn by lifting gently with a fork. Leeks stand well, but if cold weather makes the ground hard to dig, a few plants can be lifted and stored in a box of moist bark or compost until needed.

Pests and diseases: Generally trouble-free but look out for leek moth, rust, and white tip.

Other species and varieties:

'Pandora' (organic) has upright foliage and delicious, uniform, long stems and is for late summer/autumn use.

'Hannibal' is an early autumn variety that does not bulb. It has dark green leaves and a long, thick, white shank.

'St Victor' has blue/purple leaves and is very hardy for winter/spring use.

'Atlanta' has dark green foliage and straight shanks 7–9in (17–23cm) long. It has good frost resistance.

Companion plants: Carrots, celery, strawberry.

ABOVE **Leeks growing in the vegetable plot**

NAME **LETTUCE**
LACTUCA SATIVA
FAMILY **COMPOSITAE**

Type: Annual

USDA zone: All zones

Description: Lettuce is a low-growing, all-season salad plant. Leaves are usually green, but can be red or reddish-green. There are many varieties, which vary in size, form and texture. Lettuces grow best at 50–68°F (10–20°C).

Sowing and harvesting:

Late summer/autumn crop: Sow seed in late spring to mid-summer.

Early winter crop: Sow a mildew resistant variety outside in late summer. Cover with cloches in mid-autumn.

Mid-winter to early spring crop: Sow seed under glass in early to mid-autumn. Plant out when the seedlings are large enough to handle.

Late spring crop: In mild areas, sow a winter-hardy variety outside in late summer/early autumn, thin to 3in (7cm) in mid-autumn, then to 12in (30cm) in early spring. In colder areas, sow in mid-autumn under cloches for harvesting in mid-spring.

Where to grow: Lettuce likes soil that is not acid, and that has adequate organic matter incorporated. It should always be kept well watered. Summer lettuce will thrive in sun or light shade position, while spring lettuce prefers a sunny spot. Lettuce can be tucked in as a 'catch' crop, and is ideal to grow among the flowers in ornamental borders and window boxes.

How to grow: Sow seed thinly in drills ½in (12mm) deep and 12in (30cm) apart. Thin seedlings at intervals to 12in (30cm) apart, or 9in (23cm) for Tom Thumb and Little Gem. Avoid overcrowding. Water the day before thinning.

Average yield: 10–20 per 10ft (3m) row.

Maintenance: Water regularly in the morning or midday; evening watering increases the risk of disease. Ventilate glass-grown lettuce, and keep soil under the glass on the dry side.

Harvesting and storing: Harvest as soon as a firm heart has formed, or the heart will grow upward and the plants will bolt. Pull up the whole plant and cut off the root and lower leaves. Harvest loose-leaf varieties as needed, working from the outside in. Store, unwashed, in a polythene bag in the refrigerator for 3–5 days, depending on variety. Do not freeze.

ABOVE **A variety of lettuces grown singly in pots**

ABOVE **Baby lettuce 'Blush'**

Pests and diseases: Slugs and snails, root aphids, cutworm, lettuce root maggot, aphid, mosaic virus, downy mildew, botrytis.

Other species and varieties:

'Little Gem' (organic) is a quick maturing semi-cos lettuce with crisp leaves and sweet flavour.

'Buttercrunch' (organic) has a compact, dark green head and is one of the best garden varieties of lettuce.

'Tom Thumb' (organic) is a fast-growing dwarf variety.

'Saladin' (organic) is a classic 'iceberg' with large heads of shiny bright green leaves.

'Vienna' (organic) has crisp heads of a medium size. It resists mildew and leaf aphids.

'Salad Bowl' (organic) is a loose-leafed variety . It has attractive green foliage with curly edges. Two sowings will usually cover a whole season.

'Aruba' (organic) is a dark red oak-leaf variety with leaves high in vitamins A and C.

Companion plants: Beets, carrots, onions, carrots, radishes.

NAME MARROW
CUCURBITA PEPO
FAMILY CUCURBITACEAE

Type: Annual

USDA zone: 4 and above

Description: Marrows are usually trailing plants, and have green, yellow, white or striped skin.

Sowing and harvesting: Sow seed under glass in mid-spring. Plant out in early summer for harvesting from mid-summer to late autumn.

Where to grow: Marrows enjoy a well-drained soil, rich in organic matter, and need a sunny spot protected from strong winds to succeed.

How to grow: Prepare a bed by digging holes the width and depth of a spade, 24in (60cm) apart (bush) and 4ft (1.2m) apart (trailing). Fill with rotted manure mixed with soil, leaving a low mound on top. Sprinkle with an organic fertilizer before planting. To sow indoors, place a single seed edgeways and $\frac{1}{2}$in (12mm) deep in a 3in (7cm) compost-filled pot. Keep the temperature at 65°F (18°C). Harden off the seedlings before planting out. To sow outside, place 2–3 seeds 1in (2.5cm) deep and 2–3in (5–7cm) apart in the centre of each mound of the prepared bed. Thin to leave the strongest seedling at each station.

Maintenance: Keep the soil moist but water around, not over, the plants. Syringe in dry weather and mulch to conserve moisture before the fruit forms. When trailing varieties are 24in (60cm) long pinch out the main shoot tips. If the weather is cold, fertilize the female flowers by removing the male flowers, folding back the petals, and pushing them gently into the female flowers. Feed every two weeks with a liquid feed once the fruits begin to form.

Harvesting and storing: Cut the marrows where they are lying when they are 8–10in (20–25cm) long and move them away. Continual cropping prolongs fruiting. Store in a cool place.

Pests and diseases: Slugs, pollen beetles, cucumber mosaic virus.

Average yield: 4 marrows per plant.

Other species and varieties:

'Badger Cross F1' (organic) is a prolific, striped marrow of bushy habit that is resistant to cucumber mosaic virus.

'Custard White' (organic) is a patty-pan variety with an excellent flavour. Its creamy-white, circular fruits have a scalloped edge.

Companion plants: Marjoram, corn, nasturtium.

NAME MIZUNA GREENS
BRASSICA RAPA VAR. NIPPOSINICA
FAMILY CRUCIFERAE

Type: Annual/biennial depending on climate

USDA zone: All zones

Description: Mizuna is an attractive plant with shortish, slender, white juicy leaf stalks. It forms a bushy clump of feathery, glossy, green leaves.

Sowing and harvesting: Mizuna greens mature 8–10 weeks after sowing. Seedling leaves may be ready in 2–3 weeks. Sow in spring as soon as the soil has warmed up, or sow in seed trays indoors in late winter to early spring, then transplant. Harvest in summer. Outdoor sowings can continue from late spring until autumn. Harvest from late autumn on for winter use.

Where to grow: Mizuna prefers a reasonably fertile, moisture-retentive soil and grows best on an open site. Grow summer crops in light shade so they do not run to seed in hot weather. Patches look decorative in a potager or flower bed. It is also good in containers as a cut-and-come-again crop, for edgings, underplanting and intercropping.

How to grow: Sow seed indoors in trays in late winter/early spring. Thin seedlings to around 2in (5cm). Harden off and plant out in a prepared bed in spring, in block formation 2in (5cm) apart. From spring, sow seed thinly in outside rows, 2–3in (5–7cm) apart, 1/2in (12mm) deep. Thin to a minimum 1in (2.5cm) apart. For winter use, sow in rows, thin to 9in (23cm) apart and in late autumn, cover with cloches at least 8in (20cm) high.

ABOVE **Harvested mizuna greens in a garden trug**

Average yield: Up to five cuts from one plant. Plants may crop for 9–10 months.

Maintenance: Keep the soil well watered at all times as mizuna is shallow-rooted. When the plants seem to be past their best, dig them up and sow fresh seed.

Harvesting and storing: Cut leaves when they are 2–3in (5–7cm) high, leaving 1in (2.5cm) of stem to grow again. If whole heads are cut, leaving the same amount of stem, they should grow again. Freeze large leaves only.

Pests and diseases: Normally fairly trouble-free, but slugs and flea beetle can be a nuisance.

Other species and varieties:

'Tokyo Beau F1' is ideal for winter because it has a good resistance to cold.

'Kyona' is a versatile and decorative variety.

Companion plants: Marigolds, nasturtiums, marjoram, thyme.

Where to grow: In a moist, fertile soil out of direct sunlight. Both crops can be grown on a windowsill. Line containers with damp kitchen paper and sow cress four days before mustard so they mature together. Cut when they are 2in (5cm) tall. They can also be sown in sprouters.

How to grow: Broadcast or in wide drills about 3in (7cm) apart. Seedlings need no thinning.

Average yield: Variable.

Maintenance: Weed crops regularly and keep soil moist. Remove any flowering stems. Protect with cloches in winter.

Harvesting and storing: Harvest mustard as needed when the seedlings reach 1½ – 2in (3.5–5cm). Cut cress 10 days after sowing when it is 2in (5cm) high. Stems can stand for a short time in cold water, tops covered with a plastic bag.

Pests and diseases: Cabbage maggots, flea beetles, snails.

Other species and varieties:

Mustard 'Zlata' (organic) has crisp, tangy sprouts.

Cress 'Fine Curled' (organic) has fine leaves.

Companion plants: Marigolds, nasturtiums, celery, tomatoes.

NAME MUSTARD & CRESS
BRASSICA HIRTA & LEPIDIUM SATIVUM
FAMILY CRUCIFERAE

Type: Annual

USDA zone: Mustard all zones; cress zone 2 and above

Description: The seedling leaves of the cool-season crops mustard and cress are used in salads. Mustard has a sharp flavour and rapidly runs to seed in hot weather. Cress, also known as garden, curly or pepper cress, can be fine- or broad-leaved.

Sowing and harvesting: Sow in spring and autumn and harvest a few weeks later. Sow seed every 7–10 days throughout the growing season to ensure a continuous supply, but avoid sowing in hot weather.

ABOVE **Cress is a cool season crop grown for its seedling leaves**

117

NAME **OKRA (LADIES' FINGERS)**
ABELMOSCHUS ESCULENTUS
FAMILY **MALVACEAE**

Type: Tender annual

USDA zone: 5 and above, or in a greenhouse.

Description: Okra is grown for its long, green, finger-shaped edible pods. It has bright green leaves and unusual pods.

Sowing and harvesting: Sow in spring and summer for harvesting 8–11 weeks after sowing, depending on variety. Pick greenhouse-grown okra from early summer.

Where to grow: Okra prefers a fertile soil (pH6–6.5). In warm temperate and sub-tropical areas it can be grown in the open, but only in sunny conditions. It can also be grown in the greenhouse in beds or pots.

How to grow: Sow seed thinly in a seed tray or singly in small pots. The seed needs a temperature of 65–70°F (18–21°C) to germinate and should remain at this level for the whole plant-raising period. Cover with a thin layer of compost, then water. Cover the compost with a piece of glass and a sheet of newspaper. Turn the glass every day so condensation does not drop on to the seedlings. Germination will take 1–3 weeks depending on the temperature. Prick out the seedlings into 3in (7cm) pots and plant outside in early summer 21–24in (52–60cm) apart each way. Seedlings can also be planted in beds or growing bags in the greenhouse, 16in (40cm) apart. Maintain a temperature of 68°F (20°C) and humidity of more than 70 per cent and apply an organic liquid feed as recommended.

Average yield: 5–10lbs (2.3–4.5kg) per 10ft (3m) row.

Maintenance: Stake tall plants and protect from strong winds. Hoe and water regularly and mulch to retain soil moisture. Pinch out the growing points when the plants reach about 24in (60cm) tall to encourage branching. Apply a liquid feed every two weeks.

Harvesting and storing: Pick the pods when they are young and tender and the seeds are still soft. Do not allow the pods to mature because they will be unpalatable. Cut off the immature ones regularly to ensure a succession of new pods over several weeks. Wear gloves when harvesting as the pods can irritate the skin.

Pests and diseases: Aphids, caterpillars, powdery mildew.

Other species and varieties:
'Clemson Spineless' is an old variety.
'Annie Oakley' is a newer variety that may grow up to 4ft (1.2m) tall.

Companion plants: Cucumber, cauliflower, marigold, carrot.

ABOVE **Okra**

NAME ONION
ALLIUM CEPA
FAMILY ALLIACEAE

Type: Annual

USDA zone: 3 and above

Description: Onions are usually brown or yellow-skinned with white flesh, though some varieties have red skins and pinkish-white flesh. Leaf thinnings can be used like spring onions.

Sowing and harvesting: Sow seed outdoors in spring for harvesting in autumn. Sow seed under glass in late winter/early spring for cropping in late summer and autumn. Plant onion sets in early to mid-spring for harvesting in late summer.

Where to grow: Onions prefer a well-drained, reasonably fertile soil (pH6.5–7) and a sunny, sheltered site.

How to grow: Sow seed very thinly in drills ½in (12mm) deep and 9in (23cm) apart. Cover with soil. Thin the seedlings first to 1–2in (2.5–5cm) apart then to 4in (10cm) apart. Remove all thinnings to deter onion fly. Transplant seedlings raised under glass to 4in (10cm) apart in rows 9in (23cm) apart, placing the roots vertically into the planting hole and the base of the bulb about ½in (12mm) below the surface. Plant onion sets 2–3in (5–7cm) apart, or 4in (10cm) apart if larger bulbs are required, in rows 10in (25cm) apart. Only the 'nose' of the bulb should be above ground. Firm the soil around the sets.

Average yield: 8lbs (3.5kg) per 10ft (3m) row.

Maintenance: Hoe carefully or hand weed. Water only in dry weather. Feed occasionally. Stop watering once the bulbs have swollen. Mulch. Remove any flower stems that appear, and pull back the soil or mulch to allow the sun to reach the surface of the bulb.

Harvesting and storing: When the bulbs are ready to harvest, the foliage will turn yellow and topple over. Leave it for about two weeks, then lift carefully with a fork on a dry day. Spread the

ABOVE **Onions growing in the vegetable plot**

bulbs on trays and dry them for 1–3 weeks. Inspect at intervals and discard any that are damaged. When thoroughly dry, store in net bags, on trays, or tie them to lengths of cord to make onion ropes. In a cool, well-lit place, they should keep until late spring.

Pests and diseases: Onion fly, stem and bulb eelworm, saddle back, white rot, neck rot, downy mildew, shanking.

Other species and varieties:
(Seed) 'Dorato di Parma' (organic) is a late-maturing variety with large golden bulbs, ideal for long-term storage.

'Stoccarde' (organic) has well-flavoured, flat, solid bulbs and good resistance to bolting.

'Balaton' (organic) is a high-yielding variety with round, firm, dark yellow-skinned bulbs.

(Sets) 'Sturon' (organic) is a globe onion with large golden bulbs, good skin and crisp flesh.

'Red Baron' (organic) is an attractive, red skinned variety with pink and white flesh. It can be used fresh or for short-term storage.

Companion plants: Broccoli, cabbage, lettuce, strawberries, savory.

ABOVE **Welsh onions growing in the vegetable plot**

NAME **ORIENTAL MUSTARD (GAI CHOY)** *BRASSICA JUNCEA*
FAMILY **CRUCIFERAE**

Type: Hardy annuals and biennials

USDA zone: All zones

Description: Chinese mustard greens are the mild members of the mustard family. Leaf texture is blistered, deep-curled or smooth, and the leaves of some varieties are purple.

Sowing and harvesting: Sow from mid- to late summer for harvesting from autumn to spring. Oriental mustards can mature in 6–13 weeks.

Where to grow: In a rich, well-drained soil, or in containers.

How to grow: Sow in shallow drills ½in (12mm) deep and 9in (23cm) apart. When seedlings are about 2in (5cm) tall, thin to 6in (15cm) apart for harvesting young, and 14in (35cm) for larger plants. For cut-and-come again crops, sow seed thinly in drills 3in (7cm) apart and thin to about 1in (2.5cm) apart if necessary.

Average yield: Depends on the time of year and when the crop is harvested.

Maintenance: Keep well watered, and cover with cloches in autumn if hard frosts are forecast.

Harvesting and storing: Start cutting the leaves when they are 6–8in (15–20cm) high. If they grow taller, the flavour will be hot and strong. Start cutting cut-and-come again crops when the plants are 3in (7cm) high. Leave about 1in (2.5cm) of stem above ground from which new growth will develop. The large leaves can be blanched and frozen.

Pests and diseases: Relatively few.

Other species and varieties:
'Giant Red' (organic) has deep purple-red leaves in cold weather, and can reach 24in (60cm) .

'Green in Snow' is an extremely hardy winter green mustard sown in late summer to autumn.

Companion plants: Tomato, nasturtium, marigold, celery.

NAME **PAK CHOI**
BRASSICA RAPA CHINENSIS GROUP
FAMILY **CRUCIFERAE**

Type: Biennial, grown as an annual

USDA zone: 2 and above

Description: Pak choi has a loose head of fairly rigid leaves with wide mid-ribs that overlap at the base, and a mild flavour. Types vary from squat forms about 4in (10cm) tall to large plants about 18in (45cm) tall.

Sowing and harvesting: Sow under cover in early spring. Sow throughout the summer for harvesting from late summer to mid autumn. Pak choi tends to bolt from spring sowings. Mature heads may bolt if summer temperatures are high.

Where to grow: Pak choi needs a fertile, moisture-retentive soil (pH6.5–7). The soil must be able to sustain the crop's rapid growth. Plant beneath sweetcorn or between peas and beans, and sow strips between cauliflowers and Brussels sprouts. Seedling patches are useful for intercropping. Seedling pak choi and young small plants can be grown in containers.

How to grow: In drills $\frac{1}{2}$in (12mm) deep and 3in (7cm) apart for a seedling crop, 9in (23cm) apart if the plants are to mature. In dry weather, water the drills before sowing. Sow seed evenly along them, cover with a fine layer of soil and firm down gently. When the seedlings are about 4in (10cm) tall, cut the plants leaving about 1in (2.5cm) of stem to grow again. Let some of the seedlings mature, thinning to 9in (23cm) each way. If the whole crop is to grow to maturity, thin to 6in (15cm) and then to 9in (23cm).

Average yield: 10–13 heads per 10ft (3m) row.

Maintenance: Keep the plants moist at all times and use a weak liquid organic feed once a week. Mulching will help to retain moisture. Keep container plants well watered. Pak choi can be transplanted under cover in late summer for an autumn crop.

Harvesting and storing: Harvest at any stage from seedlings to the young flower shoots of the mature plants. Cut the seedling-stage crop to about 1in (2.5cm) from the soil and new leaves will sprout. Use pak choi when the leaves and leaf stalks are fresh and crisp. It does not store well, but the leaves can be dried.

Pests and diseases: Flea beetle, cutworm, slugs, cabbage caterpillar, cabbage root fly.

Other species and varieties:

'China Choi' (organic) has thick, white stems and dark green leaves. It is very uniform, slow to bolt and has good frost resistance.

'Canton Dwarf', known as Baby or Squat Pak Choi, as a compact variety that has dark green leaves and short, broad, thick white petioles.

'Pak Choi Green' is a strong variety that can be ready for harvesting six weeks after sowing.

'Shuko F1' has green stems and is slow to bolt.

Companion plants: Oregano, marigolds, nasturtium, thyme.

ABOVE **Pak Choi (white) growing in a container**

NAME PARSNIP
PASTINACA SATIVA
FAMILY UMBELLIFERAE

Type: Hardy biennial grown as annual

USDA zone: All zones

Description: Parsnips have fleshy, creamy-white edible tap roots.

Sowing and harvesting: Sow from late winter to early spring for harvesting in late autumn to early winter when the foliage dies down. Use fresh seed because older seed loses its viability.

Where to grow: Parsnips enjoy a deep, stone-free, well-cultivated soil (pH6–7) and grow well in sun or light shade. Mix well-rotted manure or compost into the soil to improve the yield and prevent the roots from forking.

How to grow: Parsnips need a soil temperature of about 45°F (7°C). They dislike cold, wet conditions. Sow seed in drills $\frac{1}{2}$–$\frac{3}{4}$in (12–18mm) deep, leaving 8in (20cm) between rows or 12in (30cm) for long-rooted varieties. Sow in groups of three seeds, 6in (15cm) apart. Thin to leave one plant per station. Put the thinnings on the compost heap, as they rarely transplant well.

Average yield: 8lbs (3.5kg) per 10ft (3m) row.

Maintenance: Hoe regularly to eliminate weeds and water frequently so the soil does not dry out. If the soil dries out and is then watered, it may make the parsnips split.

Harvesting and storing: Lift as required. Parsnips can be stored in sand, in the same way as carrots, but they tend to go soft. Alternatively, the roots can be left in the ground throughout the winter, and frost is said to improve their flavour. Lift any remaining roots in early spring so the ground is free for subsequent crops. Parsnips freeze well.

Pests and diseases: Parsnip canker, carrot fly (young seedlings). Leaf-mining celery fly can be a nuisance.

Other species and varieties:

'Tender and True' produces long roots at least 3in (7cm) across at the top, and has good resistance to canker.

'Avon Resister' produces small, even roots with round shoulders. They can be grown as little as 3$\frac{1}{2}$in (8cm) apart.

'Turga' (organic) is a traditional parsnip with wide shoulders and long tapering roots. It must be grown in deep soil.

Companion plants: Garlic, radish.

ABOVE **Parsnip seedling**

NAME **PEAS – GARDEN**
PISUM SATIVUM
FAMILY **LEGUMINOSAE**

Type: Annual

USDA zone: 2 and above

Description: Garden peas are grown for the peas in their well-filled, young pods. Put the pods on the compost heap after shelling, or use them in soups.

Sowing and harvesting: Sow from spring through summer into late autumn. Harvest in late spring to autumn. Spring sowings will crop in summer. A dwarf variety if sown in mid summer will be ready for harvesting in autumn.

Where to grow: Peas grow best in an open, sunny site. A lot of space is needed to produce them in succession, and summer crops need a deep, moisture-retentive soil. If space is limited, grow just one or two rows and pick regularly. The soil needs good structure, adequate organic matter, and enough lime to negate acidity.

How to grow: Sow seeds 3in (7cm) apart in two drills 2in (5cm) deep and 6in (15cm) apart to allow for hoeing. Press the seeds into the surface and firm down lightly after sowing.

Average yield: 10lbs (4.5kg) per 10ft (3m) row.

Maintenance: Protect from birds immediately after sowing. When the seedlings are 2–3in (5–7cm) high support with traditional pea sticks or netting. Hoe regularly to keep weeds under control. Water during dry spells in summer, and mulch to conserve moisture.

Harvesting and storing: Start picking when the pods are well-filled and the peas are small and juicy. Begin at the bottom of the stem, holding it in one hand and picking with the other, and work upwards. To promote continuous cropping, pick regularly. At the end of the season compost the stems and leave the roots in the soil. Peas freeze well.

Pests and diseases: Pea and bean weevils, pea moth, birds, mildew, mice.

Other species and varieties:

'Feltham First' is a vigorous early cropper with well-filled, pointed pods.

'Douce Provence' (organic) is a high-yielding, traditional French variety.

'Ambassador' (organic) is a robust variety with medium-sized, blunt, dark green pods. It is semi-leafless which makes picking easy.

'Kelvedon Wonder' is ideal for successional sowing. The plants are just 18in (45cm) tall.

'Sugar Pea Norli' (organic) has small, deep green pods. They have an excellent flavour and are at their best when around 2in (5cm) long.

'Ezetha's Krombek Blauwschok' (organic) has has lovely violet flowers and pods with green seeds. Eat the whole, young pods or allow to mature for use as dried peas.

Companion plants: Beans, carrots, corn, cucumber, radish, aromatic herbs.

ABOVE **Second early peas 'Early Onward'**

123

NAME PEPPER – CHILLI
CAPSICUM ANNUUM LONGUM GROUP
FAMILY **SOLONACEAE**

Type: Tender annual

USDA zone: 4 and above

Description: Chilli peppers have pointed fruit, up to 3½in (9cm) long, and attractive foliage.

Sowing and harvesting: Sow seed under cover in spring for transplanting. If grown outside, harvest before the first frosts.

Where to grow: Chilli peppers enjoy sun, shelter and a well-manured soil. They grow well in a greenhouse with a minimum temperature of 70°F (21°C) and 70–75 per cent humidity.

How to grow: Sow seed in trays in the greenhouse. Prick out seedlings into small pots. Transplant 10–12 weeks after sowing into prepared beds 18–20in (45–50cm) apart each way. Plant out when all danger of frost is over.

Average yield: 6–10 fruits per plant.

Maintenance: When the plants are established, pinch out the terminal growing points to encourage bushiness. Stake tall varieties. Water regularly, and mulch with organic matter. Feed every two weeks during the growing season, with a liquid organic fertilizer.

Harvesting and storing: Harvest chilli peppers at any stage when the colour is green to red. Harvest outside crops before the first frosts. The fruits can be stored for up to two weeks at a temperature of 54–59°F (12–15°C).

Pests and diseases: Red spider mite, aphids, blossom end rot.

Other species and varieties:

'Ring of Fire' (organic) has tapered fruits that become hotter as they change from green to blazing red.

'Marconi Rossa' (organic) has elongated fruits with a sweet, mild flavour, that turn from green to deep red when mature.

'Early Jalapeno' (organic) is an early-maturing, prolific variety with very hot, small, blunt fruits that change from dark green to red.

Companion plants: Basil, tomatoes, carrots, marjoram.

ABOVE **Organic chilli peppers 'Hungarian Wax'**

NAME PEPPER – SWEET
CAPSICUM ANNUUM GROSSUM GROUP
FAMILY **SOLONACEAE**

Type: Annual

USDA zone: 4 and above

Description: Sweet peppers can be green, cream, yellow, red, dark purple, or orange and 1½–6in (3–15cm) long.

Sowing and harvesting: Sow seed under cover in spring for transplanting. If grown outside, harvest before the first frosts.

Where to grow: Sweet peppers enjoy sun, shelter and a well-manured soil. They grow well in a greenhouse with a minimum temperature of 70°F (21°C) and 70–75 per cent humidity.

How to grow: Sow in trays in the greenhouse and prick out into small pots. Transplant into prepared beds 10–12 weeks after sowing, 18–20in (45–50cm) apart each way. Plant out when all danger of frost has passed.

Average yield: 6–10 fruits per plant.

Maintenance: Pinch out the terminal growing points of established plants to encourage bushiness. Stake tall varieties. Water regularly, and mulch with organic matter. Feed every two weeks during the growing season with a liquid organic fertilizer.

Harvesting and storing: Cut the stalk with a sharp knife about 1in (2.5cm) from the fruit. They can be stored at a temperature of 54–59°F (12–15°C) for up to two weeks

Pests and diseases: Red spider mite, aphids, blossom end rot.

Other species and varieties:

'F1 Bendigo' (organic) is a fast cropper and the first fruits are ready to harvest in late summer. The fruits are quite small and green ripening to red.

'Golden California Wonder' (organic) is very sweet and mild, with light green fruits maturing to gold-yellow.

'Jumbo' (organic) has a mild flavour and large, square fruits.

Companion plants: Basil, carrots, tomatoes, marjoram.

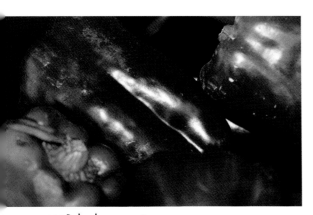

ABOVE **Red and green sweet peppers**

NAME **POTATOES**
SOLANUM TUBEROSUM
FAMILY **SOLANACEAE**

Type: Tender perennial

USDA zone: 3 and above

Description: Potatoes come in all shapes and sizes, colours and textures. Most varieties have white or pinkish-red skin and white flesh, but there are also yellow and blue-fleshed cultivars.

Sowing and harvesting: Plant first early potatoes in early spring for harvesting in the early summer. Plant second earlies in mid-spring for harvesting in mid to late summer. Plant maincrop potatoes in late spring for lifting in early to mid-autumn.

Where to grow: Potatoes can be grown in virtually every type of soil, and will help to clear new ground. They can also be grown in pots and under black polythene. They prefer a sunny position where possible and frost pockets should be avoided.

How to grow: Chit seed potatoes/tubers by placing in egg boxes with the end containing the most 'eyes' uppermost. Keep in a light, frost-free place for about six weeks until several shoots ½–1in (12mm–2.5cm) long appear. In spring, fork over the ground and rake in a general organic fertilizer. Take out 6in (15cm) deep drills, 24in (60cm) apart for early varieties and 27–30in (57–75cm) apart for later crops. Place the chitted tubers in the drills with the buds or 'eyes' upwards, 12in (30cm) apart for early varieties and 16in (40cm) apart for later crops. Cover using a draw hoe to produce mounds 4–6in (10–15cm) high over the rows.

Average yield:

Early: 12lb (5.5kg) per 10ft (3m) row.
Maincrop: 20lb (9kg) per row.

Maintenance: Hoe the furrows between the ridges regularly, and water in dry weather. When the haulms are about 9in (23cm) high, earth up to produce a flat-topped ridge about 6in (15cm) high.

Harvesting and storing:

Early varieties: When the flowers are fully open, remove a little soil carefully. If the tubers are the size of a small egg, harvest them. Using a fork, carefully lift the roots forward into the trench. Maincrop varieties: When the foliage has turned brown and the stems have withered, cut off the haulms and remove them. Wait 9–10 days, then lift the tubers and leave to dry for several hours. In a wooden box in a dark, frost-free shed, they should keep until spring. Make sure all tubers are removed from the ground.

Pests and diseases: Aphids, capsid bugs, slugs, wire worm, potato cyst, eel larva, potato blight, blackleg, soft rot, scab, wart disease

Other species and varieties:

First early: 'Epicure' (organic) is a hardy, high-yielding old variety with a floury texture and good flavour.

'Pentland Javelin' is a white-fleshed, waxy, oval variety that crops heavily and is resistant to scab and some strains of eelworm.

Second early: 'Catriona' (organic) has white-skinned, oval tubers and cream/pale yellow flesh. It crops well but cannot be stored for long periods.

'Cosmos' (organic) is waxy with bright white tubers. It is resistant to blight and common scab. Maincrop: 'Desiree' (organic) has pink skin and pale yellow flesh. It is a very heavy cropper that succeeds in all soil types.

'Lady Balfour' (organic) has oval tubers, white/pink skin and cream flesh. It is a modern variety with a high resistance to blight.

Companion plants: Beans, corn, cabbage, peas, horseradish.

ABOVE **Newly-dug 'Pentland Javelin' potatoes**

NAME **PUMPKIN**
CUCURBITA MAXIMA
FAMILY **CUCURBITACEAE**

Type: Annual

USDA zone: 3 and above

Description: Pumpkins are cultivated for their fruit and seeds. They are decorative plants, usually with a trailing habit, that are closely related to squashes, courgettes and marrows. The large, spherical fruits range from white to light yellow to golden orange. Pumpkins do best in warmer climates, but can be grown for winter use in cooler conditions.

Sowing and harvesting: Sow seed in late spring for an autumn crop.

Where to grow: Pumpkins prefer a warm, sunny position and soil enriched with plenty of manure or organic compost, about pH6.

How to grow: Sow seed inside in early to late spring, two seeds to each 3in (7cm) pot. Thin, leaving just the stronger seedling. Transplant the young plants to growing position after the last frosts in late spring/early summer. Position them about 3ft (90cm) apart in the top of prepared mounds. Alternatively, sow seed outside in late spring to early summer.

Average yield: 10–20lb (4.5–9kg) per 10ft (3m) row.

Maintenance: Weed regularly and keep the soil moist. Feed with a liquid organic fertilizer every two weeks from mid-summer to early autumn. Pinch back trailing stems at regular intervals. The fruiting laterals produce both male and female flowers, and pollination usually takes place naturally with visiting insects.

Harvesting and storing: Harvest fruits before the first frosts with a piece of stalk still attached. Dry off until the skins are hard and the fruit sounds hollow when tapped. Store in a frost-free, cool, airy place, where they will keep well.

Pests and diseases: Slugs. Mice may gnaw at the flesh of ripening pumpkins. Keep fruit off the soil to prevent rotting.

Other species and varieties:

'Small Sugar' (organic) is a widely-grown pie pumpkin with bright orange flesh and fruits up to 7in (17cm) across.

'Ghost Rider' (organic) has fruits weighing up to 20lb (9kg) and is ideal for carving.

'Baby Bear' (organic) has golden orange fruits that weigh about 3lb (1.35kg) each and are perfect for pies.

Companion plants: Sweetcorn, marjoram.

ABOVE **Pumpkin plants in flower**

NAME **RADISH**
RAPHANUS SATIVUS
FAMILY **CRUCIFERAE**

Type: Annual/biennial

USDA zone: all zones

Description: Radishes are grown for their roots and there are annual and biennial varieties. Globular varieties have roots up to 1in (2.5cm) in diameter; long forms have roots up to 6in (15cm) long. Skin colour is red, pink, white purple, black, yellow or green, depending on variety. The flesh is usually white.

Sowing and harvesting: Sow summer varieties under cloches in mid- to late winter or outdoors in the early spring for harvesting from late spring to early summer. Sow winter varieties in mid- to late summer for harvesting from mid- to late autumn on. For a long supply of radishes, sow seed every few weeks.

Where to grow: Radishes like a fertile, well-drained soil (pH5.5–6.5), preferably manured for a previous crop and with very low nitrogen levels. They should be rotated, and can be grown in a window box or a container.

How to grow: Sow summer varieties very thinly in drills ½in (12mm) deep and 6in (15cm) apart. Thin small varieties to 1in (2.5cm) apart and larger ones to 2–4in (5–10cm) apart. Sow winter varieties 9in (23cm) apart and thin to 6in (15cm). Thin all varieties before they become overcrowded. Small varieties may be used for cut-and-come again seedling leaves.

Average yield: 4lb (1.8kg) per 10ft (3m) row for summer varieties, 10lb (4.5kg) per row for winter varieties.

Maintenance: Water regularly and never allow to dry out. Protect from birds and hoe regularly to keep down weeds. Quick, uninterrupted growth is vital for a successful crop.

Harvesting and storing: Lift the roots carefully and twist off the leaves. Harvest summer varieties as soon as they are large enough or they become hot and woody. Lift winter varieties in late autumn and store in wooden boxes between layers of sand in a dry shed. They can also be left in the ground, with the crowns covered with straw, and lifted as required. Radishes will keep in a plastic bag in the refrigerator for up to a week.

Pests and diseases: Flea beetles, cabbage root maggots, cabbage root fly.

Other species and varieties:

Summer: 'Cherry Belle' (organic) is a globular variety with bright red roots, crisp white flesh, and a mild flavour.

'Scarlet Globe' (organic) is a reliable maincrop radish with bright red skin.

'Icicle' (organic) is a long variety with crisp white roots that tolerates summer heat well.

Winter: Black Spanish Round' (organic) is a black-skinned globe with crisp, white flesh.

'Rosa' (organic) is a strong-flavoured, long variety with smooth, red skin and white flesh that grows up to 6in (15cm) long.

Companion plants: Lettuce, cucumber, melons, peas, parsnip, squash, nasturtiums, chervil (which makes radishes hot).

ABOVE **A globe variety of radish**

NAME **RHUBARB**
RHEUM RHAPONTICUM
FAMILY **POLYGONACEAE**

Type: Frost-hardy perennial

USDA zone: all zones

Description: Rhubarb has large, green, frilly leaves and shiny red or pink stalks that are used like a fruit. It grows to about 24in (60cm) high, with a spread of 6ft (2m). It is a permanent crop that likes to remain undisturbed.

Sowing and harvesting: Sow seed in mid spring and plant crowns in late autumn or early spring. Do not harvest during its first year. Rhubarb can be forced under forcing jars for harvesting from early spring. Harvest the remaining plants for several weeks afterwards. Stop pulling the stems after midsummer so the plants build up reserves to survive the winter.

Where to grow: Rhubarb enjoys a sunny, open site and will grow in most soils provided that they are not subject to prolonged waterlogging in winter. It is an attractive plant that can be grown in the ornamental border.

How to grow: Dig the soil to a depth of 2ft (60cm) in late autumn or early winter, and work in a load of well-rotted manure. Skimping will reduce the yield. Rhubarb can be grown from seed or crowns but results from seed can be variable. Sow seed in a cold frame in mid spring in drills 1in (2.5cm) deep and 6in (15cm) apart. Thin seedlings to 6in (15cm apart). Set the plants in the prepared bed the following year. Plant out crowns (a piece of root with a dormant bud on top) 30in (75cm) apart in each direction for small varieties, and 4ft (1.2m) in each direction for larger varieties. Planting holes should be large enough to take the roots comfortably, and the crowns should be planted firmly with the topmost bud above the surface of the soil. Firm the soil around the plants and spread well-rotted manure over the bed.

Average yield: 6lb (2.7kg) per plant per year.

Maintenance: Keep the crowns well-watered in dry weather and mulch. Apply a heavy dressing of manure every autumn and spring. The plants need very high nitrogen levels when mature. Rhubarb usually flowers in summer. Chop out the flower bud as soon as it appears to delay flowering for a few more weeks. To force, cover the dormant buds with straw in winter. Place a forcing jar or a large container that excludes the light on top, and leave for a few weeks until the plant begins to produce young, tender stems.

Harvesting and storing: If forced, pull early stalks when they are ready and remove the jar to allow light to reach the clump. Do not force these plants again for at least two years. To harvest, hold the stalks close to the ground and pull upwards with a twisting movement. Eat only the young stalks. Rhubarb freezes well.

Pests and diseases: Flea beetles, aphids, leaf hoppers, crown rot, honey fungus.

Other species and varieties:
'Glaskin's Perpetual' is a very fast-growing variety that has green stalks tinged with red.
'Timperley Early' has thin stalks that are ideal for forcing in spring.
'The Sutton' does not run to seed and produces very large stalks.

Companion plants: Petunia, marigold and marjoram.

WARNING: Never eat rhubarb leaves. They contain oxalic acid which can be fatal.

ABOVE **Rhubarb is a vegetable that is used mainly as a fruit**

NAME **SALSIFY**
TRAGOPOGON PORRIFOLIUS
FAMILY **COMPOSITAE**

Type: Hardy biennial, grown as an annual
USDA zone: 4 and above
Description: Salsify is known as 'oyster plant' because of its flavour. Its edible, swollen tap root looks like a slender parsnip, and it has untidy green leaves and whitish-pink to mauve flowers.
Where to grow: Salsify grows best in a deep, friable, stone-free soil that has not been recently manured. It enjoys an open, sunny position.
How to grow: Sow seed in drills ½in (12mm) deep and 12in (30cm) apart. Sow two or three seeds together at 6in (15cm) intervals. Thin seedlings to one plant per station.
Average yield: 4lb (1.8kg) per 10ft (3m) row.
Maintenance: Weed carefully by hand as the roots will 'bleed' if damaged by a hoe. Water well so that the roots develop. Mulch in autumn.
Harvesting and storing: The best-flavoured roots are 10in (25cm) long and 2in (5cm) wide at the crown. They can be left in the ground in milder areas until required, although this may

encourage disease. The roots snap easily and should be lifted carefully. Tender leaves can be blanched and eaten like asparagus.

Pests and diseases: White blister.

Other species and varieties:
'Mammoth' (organic) has long tapering roots with a delicate but distinct flavour.

Sowing and harvesting: Sow seed in mid-spring for harvesting from mid-autumn. The roots are hardy and can be left in the ground until the following spring.

Companion plants: Nasturtium, lemon balm, marigolds.

ABOVE **The mauve flower of salsify**

NAME SCORZONERA
SCORZONERA HISPANICA
FAMILY COMPOSITAE

Type: Hardy perennial, usually grown as an annual
USDA zone: 4 and above
Description: Scorzonera is grown for its roots, though the young leaves and shoots or chards of overwintered plants are also edible. It has wider leaves than salsify, and long thin black roots. It also produces bright yellow flower heads. As the plants age the roots become woody.

Sowing and harvesting: Sow in mid-spring. Harvest from autumn through to spring.

Where to grow: Scorzonera prefers deep, well-drained soil (pH6–7.5), which should be stone-free so the long roots can grow unobstructed.

How to grow: Sow groups of 2–3 seeds ½in (12mm) deep and 6in (15cm) apart, in drills 12in (30cm) apart. Thin to one plant per station, discarding the weakest ones. Roots can be left in the ground to produce chards. Cover plants with 5–6in (12–15cm) of straw in early spring. The young, blanched leaves will push through. Cut when they are about 4in (10cm) tall.

Average yield: 20 roots per 10ft (3m) row.

Maintenance: Water well in dry weather. Weed regularly after germination until the leaves smother further weed growth.

Harvesting and storing: Dig the roots, which need at least four months to develop, carefully because they snap easily. Leave roots in the ground throughout the winter, or lift and store in wooden boxes in a cool place. If they are thin, leave them to thicken before harvesting the following autumn.

Pests and diseases: White blister.

Other species and varieties:
'Russian Giant' (organic) has a delicate flavour. 'Habil' has long, well-flavoured roots.

Companion plants: Marigolds, marjoram, petunias.

ABOVE **The bright yellow flower heads of scorzonera**

Sowing and harvesting: Sow in spring for harvesting in the second year.

Where to grow: Sea kale enjoys a free-draining, sandy or gravelly soil (pH6.5–7.5) and an open, sunny position. Incorporate plenty of organic matter during the autumn digging. In heavy soil it may be necessary to make a raised bed. It is suitable for flower beds and potagers.

How to grow: Sea kale can be raised from seed but will take two years to produce edible shoots. Sow in drills 1in (2.5cm) deep and 12in (30cm) apart. Thin seedlings to 6in (15cm) apart and leave until the following spring. Plant out in their permanent position. Root cuttings or thongs 3–6in (7–15cm) long are the quickest way to grow them. Take them from the fleshy side roots of plants lifted in autumn and stored in sand until the following spring. Cut one end of the thong on the slant. Place, bottom down and 1in (2.5cm) deep, 12in (30cm) apart in rows 18in (45cm) apart. Sea kale can be produced from late autumn by blanching indoors. Lift the plants from early to mid-autumn, trim off the side roots, and trim the main roots to around 6in (15cm) long. Pot up in 9in (23cm) diameter pots filled with a good compost. Allow 2 or 3 crowns per pot, and cover with an upside-down pot of the same size. Keep in total darkness at a temperature of 50–55°F (10–13°C). It should be ready for use in 5–6 weeks. Discard the forced roots afterwards.

Average yield: 10 heads per 10ft (3m) row.

Maintenance: Keep the plants well watered throughout the summer and feed with organic liquid fertilizer every fortnight. Remove any flowering shoots immediately. Cut back foliage when it begins to die in autumn. In winter, cover each crown with a plastic 9in (23cm) pot to force them. Cover the drainage holes and place straw over each pot. The blanched shoots will be ready to cut in spring.

NAME **SEA KALE**
CRAMBE MARITIMA
FAMILY **CRUCIFERAE**

Type: Hardy perennial
USDA zone: 4 and above
Description: Sea kale is grown for its leaf stems which are blanched before using. It is an attractive ornamental plant with curly, glaucous, purple leaves and a mass of honey-scented white flowers in summer.

Harvesting and storing: Begin cutting when the blanched shoots are 5–7in (13–17cm) long. Continue for 3–4 weeks.

Pests and diseases: Clubroot.

Other species and varieties: 'Lily White' is the variety usually available.

Companion plants: Celery, nasturtium, tomato, marigold.

NAME SHALLOT
ALLIUM ASCALONIUM
FAMILY ALLIACEAE

Type: Hardy perennial

USDA zone: All zones (6 for autumn planting)

Description: Shallots are grown for their edible leaves and small bulbs, milder in flavour than onions. A single bulb produces a number of offsets that develop into fully-grown bulbs.

Sowing and harvesting: Plant during early spring for harvesting in late summer. Harvest green leaves as required.

Where to grow: Shallots enjoy a light, fertile soil that should be dug in autumn. Incorporate organic matter to provide the firm ground they need. Heavy, clay soils are less suitable.

How to grow: Plant the bulbs 4in (10cm) apart in rows 12in (30cm) apart. Push individual bulbs into the soil, leaving just the tips showing. Cover with netting to prevent birds pulling them out of the ground.

Average yield: 30 bulbs per 1lb (450g)

Maintenance: Water to establish the bulbs if the spring weather is very dry, but then do not water. Weed regularly.

Harvesting and storing: When the leaves turn yellow, lift the bulb clusters, separate and allow each bulb to dry thoroughly. Remove dirt and brittle stems. Separated bulbs can be dried on an upturned crate to allow the air to circulate. Stored in a net bag in a cool, dry place, they will keep for about eight months. Bulbs can be saved for planting the following season.

Pests and diseases: Onion fly, downy mildew, onion white rot. Thrips can also be a nuisance.

Other species and varieties: 'Mikor' (organic) has round, red-gold skins, pink-tinged flesh and an average yield of 8–10 bulbs. Harvest in late summer/early autumn. 'Longor' is a mild-flavoured French shallot with long, copper-coloured bulbs and pink flesh.

Companion plants: Cabbages, carrots, lettuce, beetroot.

ABOVE **Harvested shallots**

NAME **SPINACH**
SPINACIA OLERACEA
FAMILY **CHENOPODIACEAE**

Type: Hardy annual

USDA zone: all zones

Description: True spinach is a fast-growing, green, leafy plant that looks rather like a loose lettuce. Its nutritious leaves are round or pointed, smooth or crinkled, depending on variety. It grows to 6–8in (15–20cm) with a spread of about 6in (15cm).

Sowing and harvesting: Sow seed every few weeks in early to late spring for harvesting between early summer and autumn. Sow in late summer and again in early autumn for harvesting between autumn and spring. Sow the New Zealand variety in late spring to harvest between early summer and early autumn.

Where to grow: Spinach enjoys rich, damp soil and cool conditions. Grow in short rows or small patches. It can be a useful catch crop as well as a cut-and-come-again seedling crop for use in salads. The New Zealand variety is more tolerant of hot, dry soil and poor conditions.

How to grow: In cold areas, start the first sowings under cloches. Sow individual seeds in drills 1in (2.5cm) deep and 12in (30cm) apart, or 15in (37cm) apart for New Zealand spinach seed. Thin summer varieties to 6in (15cm), winter varieties to 9in (23cm), and New Zealand varieties to 8in (20cm).

Average yield: 5–10lb (2.3–4.5kg) per 10ft (3m) row.

Maintenance: Keep well watered, and hoe regularly to remove weeds. Protect winter spinach from frost by covering with cloches from late autumn onwards. Pinch out the growing tip of New Zealand spinach to encourage the development of side shoots.

Harvesting and storing: Spinach is easy to harvest and should be picked as soon as the plants are 8in (20cm) tall. Always pick the outer leaves, which are young and tender. Harvest winter varieties sparingly. New Zealand spinach differs in that a few young shoots at the base of the plant should be pulled off during each picking session. Spinach freezes well.

Pests and diseases: Mangold fly, aphids, cucumber mosaic, downy mildew, leaf spot fungus. It can run to seed in hot, dry weather.

Other species and varieties:

'Matador' (organic) is a summer variety with large, medium green, slightly blistered leaves.

'Giant American' is a semi-erect variety with very dark green leaves, heavily blistered and rounded, for summer and autumn maturity.

'Giant Winter' (organic) is a hardy variety that stands well.

New Zealand (*Tetragonia expansa*) is a non-hardy species with smaller, fleshy leaves that is available as an organic variety.

Companion plants: Broad beans, strawberries, fruit trees.

NAME **SQUASH**
CUCURBITA MOSCHATA
FAMILY **CUCURBITAE**

Type: Tender annual

USDA zone: 11

Description: Squashes are closely related to marrows, courgettes, and pumpkins. They have spherical and globular fruits with colours ranging from yellow to green. There are two basic types: summer and winter. Summer squashes have soft skins and pale, soft flesh; winter squashes have a hard skin and fibrous, orange flesh. Both bush and trailing types are available.

Sowing and harvesting: Sow seed in spring for summer and autumn crops. Summer squash can be harvested 50–65 days after sowing. Sow outside in early summer, after the last frost, for winter crops. Winter squash can be harvested 60–110 days after sowing.

Where to grow: In humus-rich, well-drained soil in full sun. If space is limited choose a variety with bushy growth.

How to grow: Prepare a bed by digging holes the width and depth of a spade and 24in (60cm) apart for bush varieties and 4ft (1.2m) apart for trailing varieties. Fill with a mixture of rotted manure and soil, leaving a low mound on top. Sprinkle with organic fertilizer, and plant 2–3 seeds 1in (2.5cm) deep and 2–3in (5–7cm) apart in the centre of each mound. Thin to leave the strongest seedling.

Average yield: 10–80lb (4.5–36kg) per 10ft (3m) row.

Maintenance: Water regularly, but water round the plants as they are susceptible to mildew. Use a liquid organic fertilizer occasionally.

Harvesting and storing: Plant summer squashes for harvesting in warm weather when the fruits are small and tender. Store by keeping them cool and damp for 2–3 weeks. Harvest winter squashes in late autumn before the first heavy

ABOVE **Squash 'Butternut Sprinter' with flower and fruit**

frosts, when the skins are hard, cutting the thick stems to leave a 2in (5cm) stub on the fruits. Winter squash must be kept warm and dry when stored. Both types can be frozen.

Pests and diseases: Aphids, nematodes, cucumber beetles, powdery mildew.

Other species and varieties:

'Futsu' (organic) is small with a slightly ribbed, brown-orange skin, and stores for a long time if well-ripened.

'Buttercup' (organic) is a very fast-growing squash with firm, oily flesh. The dark green fruit has lighter stripes. It is shaped like a goblet.

'Butternut' (organic) stores well and has pale orange flesh.

'Delicata' is a winter 'sweet potato' squash with white skin and attractive green stripes.

'Vegetable spaghetti' (organic) is a variety with cream, oval fruits 8in (20cm) long. The flesh breaks up when boiled and looks like spaghetti.

Companion plants: Corn, onion, radish, borage, cucumber.

ABOVE **Squash 'Butternut Sprinter' in a growing bag**

NAME **SWEDE**
BRASSICA NAPUS NAPOBRASSICA GROUP
FAMILY **CRUCIFERAE**

Type: Hardy biennial, grown as annual

USDA zone: 3 and above

Description: Swedes are grown for their edible roots. They are closely related to the turnip but their flesh is usually yellow, the skin generally purple, off-white or a combination of both, and the flavour milder and sweeter. Swedes reach a height of 10in (25cm) and a spread of about 15in (38cm).

Sowing and harvesting: Sow in late spring/early summer for harvesting from early autumn onwards.

Where to grow: Swedes enjoy a sunny position in a firm, non-acid soil (pH5.5–6.5) and good drainage.

How to grow: Sow seed evenly and thinly along shallow drills ½in (12mm) deep and 15in (37cm) apart. Pull the soil back over the drills to cover the seeds. Water if the weather is dry. Thin the seedlings to 9in (23cm) apart, drawing a little soil round the base as they tend to fall over without support.

Average yield: 30lb (13.5kg) per 10ft (3m) row.

Maintenance: Hoe well to remove weeds. Water in dry weather to prevent the roots splitting.

Harvesting and storing: Lift and trim as soon as roots are large enough to use. They can be left in the ground and used as required until early spring, or lift in early winter and store them in wooden boxes in a dry, airy place.

Pests and diseases: Flea beetle, brown heart, clubroot, downy mildew, powdery mildew, violet root rot, boron deficiency.

Other species and varieties:

'Joan' (organic) can be used to grow an early crop of small to medium swedes with attractive, uniform roots.

'Willhemsburger' (organic) has a green top and pale orange flesh and is resistant to clubroot.

'Airlie' (organic) produces high yields of medium-sized roots. It has yellow flesh and a sweet flavour.

Companion plants: Nasturtium, tomato, onions, marigold, celery.

NAME **SWEET POTATO**
IPOMOEA BATATAS
FAMILY **CONVOLVULACEAE**

Type: Tender perennial, grown as annual

USDA zone: 5 and above or greenhouse

Description: Sweet potatoes are a favourite in the US. They are tropical and subtropical plants that need a temperature of 75–79°F (24–26°C) to thrive. Tuber size, shape, colour and leaf shape vary. If left unpruned, the trailing stems grow to 10ft (3m) or more.

Sowing and harvesting: Plant tubers in spring for harvesting in late summer (12–16 weeks after planting). Crops from seed are ready for lifting 20 weeks after sowing.

Where to grow: Sweet potatoes enjoy a well-drained fertile, sandy soil (pH5.5–6.5), and medium to high nitrogen levels. Grow in raised ridges about 30in (75cm) apart.

How to grow: Sow seed indoors in trays or 8–10in (21–25cm) pots at a temperature of at least 75°F (24°C). When the seedlings are 4–6in (10–15cm) high, harden them off and transplant into ridges. Alternatively, plant tubers 2–3in (5–7cm) deep and 10–12in (25–30cm) apart into ridges. Or take stem cuttings

8–10in (20–25cm) long from fully-grown plants and insert to half their length just below the highest point of the ridge.

To grow under glass, transplant seedlings when the roots have developed into prepared greenhouse beds or growing bags. Or take cuttings and insert, three to a 6in (15cm) pot. Water young plants regularly and pinch out the growing points of shoots longer than 24in (60cm) to encourage lateral shoots. Damp down regularly to keep the humidity level above 70 per cent. Ventilate the greenhouse well and maintain the temperature at 77°F (25°C). Never let it exceed 82°F (28°C).

Average yield: 8–10lbs (3.5–4.5kg) per 10ft (3m) row.

Maintenance: Weed outdoor plants regularly, water and mulch to conserve moisture. Protect from winds and train the shoots to spread around the plants. Feed both outdoor and greenhouse plants every 14–21 days until the tubers have formed.

Harvesting and storing: The tubers are ready to harvest when the stems and leaves turn yellow. Lift them carefully with a fork to prevent damage. To store, cure for 4–7 days at a temperature of 82–86°F (28–30°C) and 85–90 per cent humidity. Store in shallow trays at a temperature of 50–59°F (10–15°C). They will keep for several months.

Pests and diseases: Flea beetles, aphids, wireworm, nematodes, leafhoppers.

Other species and varieties:
'Jewel' has orange flesh.
'Gem' has white flesh.
'Nemagold' has orange flesh and is resistant to root-knot nematodes.

Companion plants: Marigolds, nasturtiums.

ABOVE **A sweet potato tuber**

NAME **SWISS CHARD**
BETA VULGARIS CICLA GROUP
FAMILY **CHENOPODIACEAE**

Type: Hardy biennial, grown as an annual

USDA zone: 5 and above

Description: Swiss chard or seakale beet is about 18in (45cm) high with broad red or white leaf stems and midribs. Leaves vary from deep green to greenish-yellow and reddish-green.

Sowing and harvesting: Sow seed in late spring. The plants usually mature 12 weeks after sowing. Harvest leaves from summer until spring when the plants may start running to seed.

Where to grow: Swiss chard prefers rich, well-manured soil and an open site, but will usually grow in any reasonable soil in either sun or light shade. It looks lovely grown in a container.

How to grow: Station-sow seed in late spring in drills ½in (12mm) deep drills, 15in (38cm) apart. When seedlings are large enough to handle, thin to 18in (45cm) apart for larger plants and 12in (30cm) apart for smaller plants.

Average yield: 7lbs (3.2kg) per 10ft (3m) row.

Maintenance: Hoe regularly to remove weeds. Water every two weeks in dry weather, and mulch to conserve moisture. Remove any flower heads that appear. Cover plants with cloches or straw in late autumn.

Harvesting and storing: The young leaves can be used like spinach. Harvest the outer leaves when young, fresh and large enough to use. Cut the stalks at the base with a sharp knife. Avoid storage if possible, as it does not keep well.

Pests and diseases: Fungal leaf spot; downy mildew. Birds sometimes attack seedlings, and slugs may attack the young plants in spring.

Other species and varieties:

'Lucullus' has yellowish-green leaves and broad yellowish-white stalks.

'Fordhook Giant' has broad, pearl-white stalks.

'Rhubarb' has bright crimson stalks and red-veined leaves.

Companion plants: Brassicas, onions, lettuce, sage, thyme, mint, dill, garlic, rosemary, hyssop.

ABOVE **Swiss chard should be eaten very fresh**

NAME TOMATO, GREENHOUSE
LYCOPERSICON ESCULENTUM
FAMILY SOLANACEAE

Type: Annual
USDA zone: 3 and above
Description: Tomatoes can be red, yellow, orange, pink or white, and spherical, plum-shaped, flat or pear-shaped. There are cherry, currant and beefsteak types, and the ribbed Marmande. Tomatoes grown in a greenhouse will produce a succession of succulent fruits.

Sowing and harvesting: In a heated greenhouse with a minimum night temperature of 50–55°F (10–13°C), sow seed in mid-winter and plant out in early spring for harvesting in early summer. In an unheated greenhouse, sow seed in early spring and plant out in late spring for harvesting in midsummer.

Where to grow: In greenhouse border beds (raised beds give better results) or in growing bags or pots. Prepare the border beds in winter. Dig in a small amount of organic material and rake in an organic fertilizer just before planting.

ABOVE **Tomatoes ripening in the greenhouse**

How to grow: Sow seed thinly in trays filled with compost and cover lightly with more compost. Keep the temperature at around 65°F (18°C) and the compost moist. Prick out seedlings into 3in (7cm) pots filled with compost and remove weaker seedlings after germination. Plant out the seedlings when they are 6–8in (15–20cm) high and the flowers of the first truss are starting to show. Or buy plants from a reputable supplier.

Average yield: 8lbs (3.5kg) per plant.

Maintenance: Water regularly to keep the soil moist and feed with a liquid feed high in potash. Too much water and feeding will reduce flavour, but too little water will cause dark sunken areas at the base of the fruits, a condition known as blossom end rot. Tie the main stems to strings suspended from overhead wires, or tie them loosely to supporting canes. Pinch out side shoots when they are around 1in (2.5cm) long. Mist with a fine spray, and tap the supports occasionally to disperse pollen and improve fruit setting. When plants are 4–5ft (1.2–1.8m) high, cut off the lower leaves up to the first truss, and remove any yellowing, decaying or diseased leaves. When plants have set six or seven trusses, remove the growing point two leaves above the top one. Shade the glass when the temperature reaches 80°F (26°C). Ventilate the greenhouse throughout the summer.

Harvesting and storing: Pick the tomatoes when they are ripe and fully colourful, with the calyx still attached. At the end of the season ripen green fruits in a layer on a tray placed in a drawer, or cut the strings and lay the plants on a bed of straw, then cover with cloches.

Pests and diseases: White fly, potato mosaic virus, grey mould (botrytis), seedling blight, magnesium deficiency, boron deficiency, foot and root rots, blossom end rot, tomato leaf mould.

Other species and varieties:

'Moneymaker' (organic) is a popular variety with large trusses of medium-sized fruit.

'Alicante' (organic) is an early cropper with a good flavour.

'Yellow Perfection' is a very early and prolific with smooth, round, golden-yellow fruits.

Beefsteak varieties: 'Ultra Boy' is an F1 variety with large globular fruits.

'Dombito' has good disease resistance and fruits that weigh around 12oz (350g).

Companion plants: Basil, sage, parsley, nasturtiums, French marigolds.

ABOVE **A banana can be hung from the stem of a tomato plant to help the ripening process**

NAME **TOMATO, OUTDOOR**
LYCOPERSICON ESCULENTUM
FAMILY **SOLANACEAE**

Type: Tender annual

USDA zone: 3 and above

Description: Outdoor tomato crops have more flavoursome fruits and, if bush varieties are grown, are less hard work. They do not grow well at temperatures below 61°F (16°C) and do not tolerate frost, so in many areas extra protection will be needed. Choose a variety recommended for outdoor growing.

Sowing and harvesting: Sow under glass in early spring. Plant young seedlings out in early summer, after all danger of frost has passed. Harvest in late summer.

Where to grow: Tomatoes enjoy a warm spot in front of a south-facing wall and a rich, deep, fertile soil with plenty of organic matter worked in. They will not tolerate cold or wind, so a netting windbreak is a good idea. They can be grown in 9in (23cm) pots or growing bags. Some varieties are good in hanging baskets and window boxes.

How to grow: Sow seed ¾in (18mm) deep at a temperature of 59°F (15°C) in compost-filled seed trays. Transplant seedlings at the two- or three-leaf stage into 2–3in (5–7cm) pots, giving them plenty of light, space and ventilation. Harden off the young plants, and plant outside when the flowers on the lower truss can be seen.

Average yield: 4lbs (1.8 kg) per plant.

Maintenance:

Cordon varieties: As the plants grow, tie the main stem loosely to a cane at 12in (30cm) intervals. When small tomatoes have developed on the fourth truss, remove the growing point two leaves beyond it. Remove side shoots that appear where the leaf stalks join the main stem when they are about 1in (2.5cm) long. Remove yellowing, damaged and diseased leaves below the fruit trusses as the growing season progresses, but do not overdo this process. Water regularly and evenly to keep the soil moist and feed regularly with a high-potash liquid feed. Over-watering and overfeeding can cause loss of flowers.

Bush varieties: Plant 12–36in (30–90cm) apart, depending on variety. They tend to sprawl on the ground. Do not remove side shoots. Dwarf varieties can be spaced more closely. Cover with cloches in the early stages of growth.

LEFT **Many varieties of tomato can be grown successfully outdoors**

Harvesting and storing: Pick the fruits when ripe. The earliest bush varieties can be harvested 7–8 weeks after planting. Hanging a banana from the stem will help the ripening process. Ripen green tomatoes by placing a layer of fruit on a tray and storing in a drawer, or lay the plants on a bed of straw and cover with cloches.

Pests and diseases: Leafhopper, potato cyst eelworms, tomato blight, and damping-off in seedlings.

Other species and varieties:
Cordon (grown as single stems):
'Saint Pierre' (organic) has deep red fruits, high yields and a good flavour.
'Outdoor Girl' is a heavy cropper with slightly ribbed, well-flavoured fruits and is one of the earliest tomatoes to ripen.
'Gardener's Delight' (organic) is a popular variety that produces a heavy crop of bite-sized tomatoes with a tangy flavour.
'Marmande' (organic) has large, irregular shaped, fleshy fruits with few seeds and a rich flavour.
Bush:
'Tiny Tim' is a dwarf bush with bright red, cherry-like fruit, that is ideal in window boxes.
'Tumbler' is a trailing variety with prolific crops of bright red fruit, suitable for containers and hanging baskets.
'Totem F1' has a dwarf, compact habit suited to growing in pots and window boxes.

Companion plants: Cabbage, carrots, celery, onion, mint.

NAME TURNIP
BRASSICA CAMPESTRIS RAPIFERA GROUP
FAMILY CRUCIFERAE

Type: Hardy biennial
USDA zone: all zones
Description: Turnips are grown for their edible roots, which are not as sweet as the roots of swedes, and for their bunching green tops.
Sowing and harvesting: Turnips are usually ready to harvest 6–12 weeks after sowing. Sow early varieties in spring, and make successive sowings at three-week intervals until early summer for harvesting during summer/early autumn. Sow maincrop varieties where they are to grow in mid/late summer for cropping and storage from mid-autumn onwards. Sow maincrop varieties in early autumn for spring greens the following spring.
Where to grow: Sow early varieties in a well-manured, fertile soil. Maincrop and storage varieties need a reasonably well drained, non-acid, firm soil (pH6.5 or above), and a fairly sunny position. Dig the soil in autumn and prepare a seedbed in spring. The roots will fork if grown in freshly-manured soil, so if possible use a site that has been well manured for a previous crop.
How to grow: Sow the earliest crops under glass in late winter at a temperature of 65°F (18°C). Harden off the young plants before planting out under cloches 12in (30cm) apart. Alternatively, you can sow seed outside in shallow drills 12in (30cm) apart. Thin the seedlings when they are large enough to handle to 9in (23cm) apart for maincrop varieties or 6in (15cm) apart for early varieties.
Average yield:
Early varieties: 7lb (3.2kg) per 10ft (3m) row.
Maincrop varieties: 12lb (5.4kg) per row.

Maintenance: Keep the crop weed free, and water as necessary. The roots will become woody if they are allowed to dry out at any stage. Mulch with well-rotted compost or manure to avoid tough roots.

Harvesting and storing: Cut the turnip tops when they are about 5in (12cm) high, and leave in the ground to re-sprout. Pull the roots of early varieties when they are the size of a tennis ball. Lift maincrop turnips with a fork as soon as they are large enough to use. They can also be left in the ground and harvested as required, but their tenderness and flavour decrease with age. In cold, wet areas, lift the roots in late autumn and twist off the tops. Place them between layers of dry peat or sand in a wooden box and store in a cool, airy place.

Pests and diseases: Turnip gall weevil, aphids, cabbage root fly, turnip mosaic virus, black rot, soft rot.

Other species and varieties:
Early: 'Purple Top Milan' (organic) has roots that are white below the soil and purple above, and is quick to mature.

'Snowball' is a fast-growing, globular, white-fleshed variety best eaten when very young.

Maincrop: 'Golden Ball' (organic) has round, golden roots with tender yellow flesh and excellent keeping qualities.

'Noir d'Hiver (organic) is a fast-maturing winter variety with cylindrical, black-skinned roots.

Companion plants: Marigold, nasturtium, celery, tomato, onion.

ABOVE **Baby turnips 'Arcoat'**

NAME **WATERCRESS**
RORIPPA NASTURTIUM-AQUATICUM
FAMILY **CRUCIFERAE**

Type: Hardy aquatic perennial

USDA zone: 3 and above

Description: Watercress has beautiful green, hot, tangy leaves that are used in salads and soups. Its natural habitat is freshwater streams.

Sowing and harvesting: Sow in late spring for harvesting at the end of the summer onwards.

Where to grow: Watercress needs a rich, fertile, moisture-retaining soil, and prefers a position out of direct sunlight – a spot in a shaded, damp area is ideal. It can be grown as a cut-and-come-again seedling crop, and is suitable for container growing.

How to grow: Dig a trench 12in (30cm) wide and 12in (30cm) deep, incorporating lots of organic matter into the bottom. Put a 6in (15cm) layer of organic matter on top and fill the rest of the trench with soil. Scatter the seed over the trench and cover with a sifted layer of soil. Thin seedlings to 4in (10cm) apart each way to form a block. To grow from plants, plant rooted shoots 4in (10cm) apart each way to form a block. They will soon spread to form a solid mat.

Average yield: Depends on the time of year and the stage at which you harvest.

Maintenance: Keep plants well-watered at all times. In warm weather this should be twice a day. Clip back to maintain a bushy habit, and cut off the flower stems as soon as they appear.

Harvesting and storing: Harvest leaves as required, but do not remove too many in the first year because it will weaken the plants. Pick the stems regularly to encourage new growth. Cut off the base of the stems, remove discoloured leaves and wash the stems thoroughly. Shake off any remaining water. Watercress can be kept in a polythene bag in the refrigerator for a couple of days.

Pests and diseases: Flea beetles, snails.

Other species and varieties: No named varieties available.

Companion plants: Carrot, radish, spinach, strawberry, onion.

ABOVE **A basket of fresh vegetables**

CHAPTER 6

Companion plants

Companion plants can play a vital part in the running of an organic garden. They can be used to keep away pests, or to attract insects that will literally eat up the problem. They are especially good in the vegetable garden, where they are can be as beautiful as they are useful. A well-planned plot that includes colourful companion plants can look as good as any herbaceous border. The selection of plants featured is by no means comprehensive, but it should help you choose what to grow with some of the vegetables listed. If it whets your appetite, there are numerous books on the subject.

ABOVE **Mixed bed of herbs and flowers**

PLANT LIST

BASIL

ABOVE When it is planted with tomatoes, basil helps to improve their growth and flavour

CHAMOMILE

ABOVE Chamomile is often called 'the plants' physician' because it helps to protect them against various pests and diseases

BORAGE

ABOVE Borage is a magnet for bees and is a good a companion plant to tomatoes and squash because it deters tomato worm

CHIVES

ABOVE Chives are good companion plants for beetroot, tomatoes and carrot because they deter aphids and improve growth and flavour

CLOVER

ABOVE Clover has long been used as a green manure plant and also as a companion because it attracts many of the beneficial insects

FRENCH MARIGOLDS

ABOVE The roots of French marigolds exude a substance that spreads into the soil nearby and kills off nematodes

CORIANDER

ABOVE Coriander is a companion to potatoes because it deters aphids and attracts bees

GARLIC

ABOVE Garlic is a good companion to celery, radishes and parsnips because it has a pungent smell that deters aphids

HYSSOP

ABOVE Hyssop is a good companion plant to Brussels sprouts and cabbage because it deters cabbage moths

LEMON BALM

ABOVE Dried, powdered lemon balm sprinkled throughout the garden will deter many pests

LAVENDER

ABOVE Lavender's flowers attract many beneficial insects, and it is a good companion plant to chicory

MARJORAM

ABOVE Marjoram's scent confuses pests, and it is a good companion plant to spring onions, sweetcorn, pumpkins, courgettes, mizuna greens, aubergines and sweet peppers

MINT

ABOVE Mint is a good companion to cabbage and tomatoes because it deters pests including cabbage moths, ants and aphids

OREGANO

ABOVE Oregano is a good grown near cauliflower and pak choi because it improves their flavour and repels cabbage butterflies

NASTURTIUM

ABOVE Plant nasturtiums between plants because they help to minimize pests by attracting beneficial insects

PARSLEY

ABOVE Plant parsley among tomatoes and asparagus because it attracts bees as well as hoverflies

PETUNIA

ABOVE Plant petunias throughout the garden as they repel many garden pests

POT MARIGOLDS

ABOVE Grow pot marigolds to attract beneficial insects such as hoverflies and bees into the garden

POACHED EGG PLANT

ABOVE Poached egg plants are a good companion plant for tomatoes because they attract hoverflies which devour aphids

POPPIES

ABOVE Poppies are good grown near many plants, and they attract lacewings which love to eat aphids

ROSEMARY

ABOVE Rosemary is a good companion plant for brassicas because it deters cabbage moths, bean beetles and carrot flies

SOUTHERNWOOD

ABOVE Southernwood is a good companion plant to cabbages because it deters cabbage butterflies

SAGE

ABOVE Sage is a good companion plant to carrots and cabbages because it deters carrot fly and cabbage moth

STRAWBERRIES

ABOVE Strawberries are good companions to cabbage, leeks, lettuce and onions

SUNFLOWER

ABOVE Sunflowers are good when planted among sweet corn, and are believed to increase the yield

THYME

ABOVE Thyme is good with most vegetables, particularly cabbage, cauliflower and pak choi because it strengthens the plants, repels aphids and deters cabbage worms

TANSY

ABOVE Tansy is a good companion to cauliflower because it repels flying insects and ants

TOBACCO PLANT

ABOVE Grow tobacco plants in the greenhouse to encourage parasitic wasps, which control whitefly larvae

Glossary of gardening terms

ACID
With a pH value of less than 7. Acid soil is deficient in lime. with few basic minerals.

ALKALINE
With a pH value of more than 7. Chalk or limestone soil is usually alkaline, and most herbs will thrive in it.

ANNUAL
A plant grown from seed that germinates, flowers, seeds and dies in one growing season.

ANTHER
The part of the stamen that contains the pollen.

BIENNIAL
A plant that completes its life cycle in two years. It produces stems and leaves in the first year, flowers in the second, then sets seed and dies.

BLANCHING
The process of withholding light from a plant to prevent the development of chlorophyll.

COLD FRAME
An unheated structure with a glass or plastic cover, used to protect plants in winter.

COMPOST
1 A growing medium containing ingredients such as peat, loam, sand and leaf mould, in which seeds are sown and plants potted.
2 Recycled, decomposed plant material and other organic matter used as a soil improver and as a mulch.

CROCKS
Broken pieces of clay pot used in the bottom of a container to improve drainage and provide air circulation to the root system of plants.

CROWN
The basal part of a herbaceous perennial, at or just below the surface of the soil, from which the roots and shoots grow.

CULTIVAR
A variety of plant that has been cultivated, rather than one that grows naturally in the wild.

CUTTING
A piece of stem, root, shoot, bud or leaf cut from the parent plant, used to grow more specimens.

DEAD HEAD
Remove spent flowers or flower heads to encourage further growth/another flowering, and to prevent self-seeding.

DECIDUOUS
Plants that lose their leaves at the end of the growing season. They are renewed at the start of the next growing season.

DIVISION
A method of increasing plants in which dormant roots are divided into two or more parts.

DORMANCY
Resting period of a seed or plant, usually in winter, where there is a temporary slowing or cessation of growth.

DRILL
A straight furrow made in the soil for sowing seed in a line.

EVERGREEN
Plants, mostly shrubs and trees, that keep their leaves all year round, though some older leaves are lost regularly throughout the year.

FORCING
The process of making a plant grow or flower before its natural season, usually done by increasing temperature.

GERMINATION
Changes that take place as a seed starts to grow and the root and shoot emerge.

GROUND COVER
Low-growing plants that cover the ground quickly and suppress weeds.

HABIT
Characteristic shape and appearance.

HALF-HARDY
Plants that will over-winter successfully outdoors in a sheltered position. They may not survive severe frosts.

HARDENING OFF
A technique for acclimatizing plants to outside temperatures. Place them outside during the day for increasing periods and put them back under cover at night. This can take two or three weeks.

HARDY
Plants that can survive the winter outdoors, including frosty conditions, without protection.

HERBACEOUS
Plants, usually with non-woody stems, that die down at the end of each growing season.

HUMUS
Crumbly, dark brown, decayed vegetable matter formed when plant remains are partially broken down by bacteria.

HYBRID
A plant created from parents of different species or genera.

INVASIVE
A vigorous plant that will suffocate neighbouring plants if not controlled or grown in a container.

LANCEOLATE
Term used to describe a leaf shaped like a narrow spear that tapers at each end.

LAYERING
Method of propagation in which a stem is pegged down into the soil and encouraged to root while still attached to the parent plant.

LIME
Compounds of calcium. The proportion of lime in a soil determines whether it is acid, neutral or alkaline. Some soils are predominantly lime.

LOAM
Soil composed of an even mixture of clay and sand, with a balanced mixture of nutrients. Loam is well-drained, fertile and retains moisture well.

MULCH
A layer of material applied to the surface of the soil to improve its structure, conserve moisture, protect roots from frost, and suppress weeds.

NODE
The point on a stem from which leaves, shoots, branches or flowers arise.

NUTRIENTS
Minerals used to develop proteins and other compounds necessary for healthy plants.

OVATE
Term used to describe egg-shaped leaves that are broad at the base, and pointed at the tip.

PEAT
Partly-decayed organic matter with a water-retaining structure used in composts or mulches. Peat substitutes like coconut fibre may be used.

PERENNIAL
A plant, usually herbaceous, that lives for at least three seasons. It flowers each year, dies down in winter, and new shoots appear each spring. Woody-based perennials die down only partly.

pH
A scale that indicates soil alkalinity or acidity.

PINCHING OUT
Removal of a plant's growing tips to encourage side-shoots. Also known as 'stopping'.

PINNATE
Term for leaflets arranged in pairs on either side of the stem, usually opposite each other.

PRICK OUT
Transfer seedlings from the bed or container where they germinated to pots or areas of the garden where they will have room to develop.

PROPAGATION
Increasing plants vegetatively or by seed.

PROSTRATE
Growing low or flat over the ground.

RACEME
Short lateral stalk springing from a central stem. Clusters of separate flowers are attached.

RHIZOME
A branched underground stem that bears roots and shoots.

RUNNER
A slender, horizontally spreading stem that runs along the surface of the soil, rooting at intervals.

SELF-SEEDING
Term for plants that shed seeds around them after flowering, from which new plants grow.

SPECIES
Plants of a specific type and constant character that breed together.

TAP ROOT
The long, strong, main root of a plant that grows downwards into the soil.

TENDER
Plants susceptible to damage at low temperatures that cannot survive outside during winter.

TILTH
Ideal, fine, crumbly, soil broken down into small crumbs by correct digging and raking.

TOPSOIL
The fertile, upper layer of soil.

TRIFOLIATE
Consisting of three leaflets.

UMBEL
Flat-topped or rounded flower cluster on a flower stalk, radiating from a central point.

VARIETY
Term for a variant of an original species or hybrid, often used to describe cultivars.

WHORL
Three or more leaves or flowers forming a ring at one stem joint.

Index

GMC Publications Ltd,
166 High Street, Lewes, East Sussex BN7 1XU, United Kingdom
Tel: 01273 488005 Fax: 01273 402866
E-mail: pubs@thegmcgroup.com
www.gmcbooks.com

Contact us for a complete catalogue, or visit our website